28 PORTUGUESE POETS

A BILINGUAL ANTHOLOGY

28 PORTUGUESE POETS

A BILINGUAL ANTHOLOGY

Edited, with an Introduction, by Richard Zenith

Translated by Richard Zenith and Alexis Levitin

DEDALUS PRESS
DUBLIN, IRELAND

First published in 2015 by
The Dedalus Press
13 Moyclare Road
Baldoyle
Dublin 13
Ireland

www.dedaluspress.com

ISBN 978 1 910251 00 3

Dedalus Press titles are represented in the UK by Inpress Books (www.inpressbooks.co.uk).

Typesetting: Patrícia Cálão & Pat Boran
Cover image © Carlos Botelho, SPA 2014

FUNDED BY THE DIREÇÃO-GERAL DO LIVRO, DOS ARQUIVOS E DAS BIBLIOTECAS

THE DEDALUS PRESS RECEIVES FINANCIAL ASSISTANCE FROM THE ARTS COUNCIL / AN CHOMHAIRLE EALAÍON

CONTENTS

Nuno Júdice

Ana Luísa Amaral

Adília Lopes

Paulo Teixeira

INTRODUCTION

IN THE 36TH POEM from *The Keeper of Sheep*, Alberto Caeiro makes fun of poets who assemble their verses like a carpenter his boards or a bricklayer his bricks, "making sure each one is right, and taking it away if it isn't!" Against a poetics of careful construction, he says that poems should take shape in the same natural way that flowers grow and blossom. He has no use for poems conceived as buildings made of words, since "the only true house is the whole Earth". Celebrating all things as they are immediately perceived by the five senses, Caeiro claimed to be "Nature's only poet". For shelter against the rain and cold, he lived in a simple white house on top of a hill.

Or perhaps half way up the hill. Fernando Pessoa — Portugal's greatest Modernist poet — was undecided about where exactly to place the dwelling of Caeiro, an alter ego he invented in March of 1914. The shepherd-poet's white house is mentioned in more than one poem, but its location on the hill varies. Several months after engendering bucolic Caeiro, Pessoa invented the classicist Ricardo Reis and the urbane naval engineer called Álvaro de Campos, all of whom wrote in very different styles and with different points of view about poetry, religion, politics, and how to live. Pessoa called these fictional poets "heteronyms", endowed them with individuated biographies, and even cast their astrological charts.

Fernando Pessoa, unlike Caeiro, was a constructor. He was wary of spontaneous, unmediated expression and would have appreciated the Brazilian poet João Cabral de Melo Neto (1920-1999), whose second book of poems was pointedly titled *O Engenheiro* [The Engineer]. In a poem written some time after the death of Marianne Moore (1887-1972), Melo Neto praised her work for showing

> that poetry is not on the inside
> but is, like a house, something outside,
> and before one lives inside it

it must be built — this something
one makes to make oneself able,
this crutch for the one who is lame.

He broadly divided poets into bleeders, whose writing is an overflow of what they intensely feel, and crutch poets like himself, who write to compensate for what they lack in feeling.

Pessoa, who assumed that all poets feel intensely, divided the waters of poetry along somewhat different lines. He distinguished between those who disclose their feelings directly, in their natural, unprocessed state, and those who convert feelings into an impersonal poetic construction. His byword for the latter method was *fingimento*, which means pretending, feigning, forging — not in the sense of lying or counterfeiting but in the sense of inventing and dramatically representing.

"Here I'm not" vs. "Here I am"

Fernando Pessoa was a hard-core, proselytizing *fingidor*, since to reproduce in poetry what already exists in reality seemed to him a trivial ambition and since we don't really know what, in reality, exists. Even Alberto Caeiro, the one great moment of spontaneity and directness in Pessoa, admits to being a pretender in the opening verses of *The Keeper of Sheep:*

I've never kept sheep
But it's as if I kept them.

Álvaro de Campos, after years of voyaging around the world, living in various countries and doing his best to "feel everything in every way possible" (his motto), begins a poem with this ironic discovery: "I'm beginning to know myself. I don't exist." In the world according to Pessoa, there were no certainties. Everything was as if. It was not just to have fun with us, or with literature, that he divided himself into alter egos — including several dozen lesser heteronyms who wrote poetry and prose in

Portuguese, English and even French; it was because the notion of a coherent, solid-state I struck him as an illusion. No one is today what he or she was yesterday. We are in permanent flux.

While Pessoa quietly produced a diversified literary oeuvre founded on doubts about the nature of the world's and his own existence, Florbela Espanca wrote an exalted poetry that simply and insistently proclaimed "I am!" She also had her doubts, but she battled rather than indulge them. The battle was partly motivated, or necessitated, by her gender. Although there were plenty of women poets in Portugal, they were rarely taken seriously by the literary establishment, and Espanca — one of the few Portuguese women of her day to attend university — was taken only half seriously. She was considered the best of the female lot of poets, insofar as her well-made sonnets were a little less "female", able to be measured against the poetry written by men. Still, she was emotive and effusive, she used a lot of exclamation marks, and to this day her poetry is disregarded by some of the literature programmes at Portuguese universities. I too did not pay it much regard, I never really read it closely, until a scholar of Espanca's sonnets asked me to translate a group of them for a book she was co-authoring. Although the themes, images and technical features of her sonnets are not especially remarkable, I was impressed by the unusual concentration of feeling that they contain, or rather, consubstantiate. Without Alberto Caeiro's discourse but as if following his recommendations, this poet took the whole world to be her house, and her sonnets are like large poetic flowers that seem to be generated organically. She is no poet of Nature, however. Hers is an unabashed song of the self.

The highly personal, subjectively expressive Espanca, who was born six years after Pessoa and died five years before him, probably from suicide, makes for a radical contrast with his poetics of impersonalization, but in the short run she had no influence. And the Pessoan performance, with its cast of diverse heteronyms, was a hard act to follow. In fact almost no poet with brio emerged in the last years of Pessoa's life or in the years immediately after his death, in 1935. The most notable exception was Vitorino Nemésio (1901-1978). Deftly fusing images and scenes from his Azorean childhood and travels abroad with an impressive philosophical and literary erudition acquired in his university studies on the Portuguese mainland, Nemésio was a restlessly versatile, somewhat isolated virtuoso. (His exclusion from this anthology is due to my failure to produce translations of his poems that satisfy me.)

The post-Pessoa diversity

The years during and after World War II saw a fresh flowering of Portuguese poets, who dealt with the dazzling and potentially intimidating legacy of Pessoa in different ways. Nearly all of them learned something from Pessoa, but only one of the poets presented here — the protean Jorge de Sena, who was also a novelist, playwright and literary critic — seems to have been in competition with him. Although he applied the lesson of *fingimento* for transforming personal feeling into material suitable for making works of art, Sena also countered it with a poetics of witness and testimony linked decisively to real life. His large output of poetry varied considerably from book to book, but without ever straying far from his concern for what it means to be individually, collectively and sexually human. One of the early and most illuminating interpreters of Pessoa's work, he devoted even more pages of criticism to the great Renaissance poet Luís de Camões (1524-1580), who was arguably the antithesis of Pessoa. An adventurer not only in his literary imagination but also in the flesh, Camões was a rapacious lover of life, with all the beauty, squalor, joy and violence it contains. Pessoa kept the world at arm's length. Sena shared Pessoa's taste for intricately intellectual pursuits, but he also — like Camões — spent his adult life on three different continents and whole-heartedly embraced the world and the experience of love. His "My Desired Tomb", with its seeming endorsement of sexual abuse and exploitation, might strike some as politically or socially incorrect, but it is actually a marvellous hymn to life itself.

Life itself was also at the centre of Sophia de Mello Breyner's poetic project, and in her case "life" included a manifestly spiritual dimension. Pessoa is the subject of several of her poems, and she wrote a series of seven odes in the style of Ricardo Reis, but she had a different take on the world's endless multiplicity and the fragmented self. "Nature is parts without a whole", Pessoa ventriloquized through Alberto Caeiro, and he considered unity to be possible only in a work of art or a literary composition, and perhaps in a hazy spirit dimension that could not be directly apprehended. Sophia Breyner erased the distance between heaven and earth. God, or the gods, coexist with humans in her poetry, which used myth and mythology to suggest ways to repair a broken order, to connect the drama of the individual to the universal scheme of things — not only on the written page but in the life we all live. Her poetry sometimes has an oracular quality, with the verses demanding to be read aloud, one vatic word after another, and darkness and pain have their arcane, inevitable place in the luminous world those verses announce. The sea of Crete in which she swims, and which represents "primordial joy", is also where the Minotaur "darkly moves" (p. 63). There is nothing facile about her world view or religious faith.

Carlos de Oliveira's "Stalactite", a poem in 24 sections (only the first seven are presented here), is from a collection titled *Micropaisagem* [Microlandscape], and it's as if this poet used language as a microscope for seeing into things. His writing developed in the context of the Portuguese neo-realist movement, which emerged in the 1940s as a reaction to literature that failed to address the deplorable social and political conditions of a poor nation ruled by the claustrophobic regime of Salazar, and his five novels more obviously reflect the agenda of that movement. But Oliveira, along with certain other neo-realists, did not only critique capitalism and oppose tyranny; he also called into question entrenched forms of conceiving and making art, and particularly the individualistic consciousness as the centre point of literary productions. His novels anticipate the preoccupation of the French nouveau roman with objects and environments for their own sake, and this focus on objective reality is even more extreme in his poetry, where words seem almost inseparable from the things they describe. Or is it things that define words?

Oliveira's stalactite, finally, is the poem itself.

Like Sena and Oliveira, Eugénio de Andrade published his first book of poetry in 1942. (Breyner's first book saw print two years later.) The locus of his poetic investigations is the human body. It is a musical, sensual and glowing body, which walks through all the seasons and all weathers. The sun prevails, but this poetry is not only about illuminated vision. It engulfs the reader through all the senses: sight, smell, sound, taste, and touch. Andrade travelled to Greece with Sophia de Mello Breyner, whose observations of an ancient sculpture of Antinous or of a contemporary Greek workman muscularly negotiating a bulldozer (pp. 59 and 61) inspired poetic contemplations on the divine element in humanity. Andrade's observations of male bodies inspired poems that are idealized, exquisitely sensorial evocations of the body itself, or of the body and its aura.

Mário Cesariny was the most prominent poet of Portugal's late-blooming surrealist movement, founded in 1947. It was partly an exasperated response to the neo-realist movement, whose Marxian correctness came to feel like a new form of despotism for writers interested in other things besides economic reform and class struggle. An openly practising homosexual who was arrested more than once for immoral conduct, Cesariny insisted on the freedom to speak his mind and act on his desires. The obstacles to that freedom are powerfully evoked in "you are welcome to elsinore", where the Danish town made infamous by Shakespeare represents the Salazar regime but also human duplicity and small-mindedness. To produce poems such as "The ship of mirrors", Cesariny claimed to rely on the automatic writing method advocated by the French surrealists for bypassing the rational mind and connecting to the subconscious. But it was with the full use of his conscious mind that he dedicated an entire book of poems to parodying and deconstructing Fernando Pessoa and his heteronymic system, suggesting — on one level — that the great Modernist was too abstractly clever and sexually pent-up for his own good; on another level, the unruly surrealist wanted to shake up all that we his readers hold to be dear and sacred, including our literary monuments.

The poet Alexandre O'Neill introduced Cesariny to the writings of André Breton and other French surrealists, but after collaborating for several years with the Portuguese version of surrealism, he went his own way. He was suspicious of anything remotely mystical, including automatic writing's hotline to the subconscious, but he shared Cesariny's attitude of permanent revolt against convention and all forms of censorship. He thought that his fellow countrymen were far too well behaved, and he deliberately used a traditional, metrically obedient sonnet to indict them for taking comfort in a mythified past rather than rebelling against present oppression (in "Standing at Fearful Attention"). He was no cultivator of Portuguese *saudade*, a supposedly unique feeling of deep longing, yearning, nostalgia. Systematically sceptical, critical, and ironic when not downright sarcastic, O'Neill also had a profoundly tender side, which he indulged with caution.

António Ramos Rosa, astonishingly prolific, published dozens of books over the course of more than five decades. Although his work naturally evolved — early on he produced some notable poems of social protest — the lexicon, colouring and music of his mature style are remarkably consistent, to the point of obsessiveness. The six poems published here are all from *The Book of Ignorance* (1988), which is a meditation on and search for "animal intelligence", explicitly invoked at the end of the poem "Sometimes the middle of a grove". Another poem, "Calmness extends as we get old", affirms that we "can know nothing / by way of analysis", and the almost monotonic flow of this poet's verses reads to me like a Gregorian or Buddhist chant seeking to know — to penetrate — the heart of the world by way of an intensely focused verbal perseverance. The words are like polished pebbles now rolling, now pausing, on the bed of a pellucid stream.

1961: a heterogeneous generation

Herberto Helder and Ruy Belo published their first books of poetry in 1961, and five other young poets — including Luiza

Neto Jorge and Fiama Hasse Pais Brandão — published chapbooks in a magazine called *Poesia 61.* It was also an important year in the political sphere, with wars for independence breaking out in several of Portugal's African colonies. The colonial wars, which soon spread from Angola and Guinea Bissau to Mozambique, aroused strong international and internal opposition, even within the Portuguese army itself, and hastened the downfall of Salazar's Estado Novo, or New State, which continued to rule the country for six years after ill health forced the prime minister to step aside, in 1968 (he died in 1970). Although some poems were made into effective song lyrics for a swelling protest movement, the wars and the latter decades of the dictatorial regime did not give rise to a significant body of political poetry. It must be stressed that the regime had little in common with the autocratic governments in Eastern Europe. The Portuguese could move about freely, censorship existed but information was not strictly controlled, and the State did not run the economy. The secret police monitored all political activity, however, and the climate was stifling for intellectuals and artists, many of whom left the country. (Many other people left in search of better paying jobs.) It is possible that some young Portuguese were attracted to poetry as a place of exile, but this is an attraction that always applies, regardless of one's personal or collective situation. Perhaps it was merely by chance that a cluster of good poets born and raised under the same political system began publishing at around the same time. Not united by any poetic programme, the one point in common for most but not quite all of these poets is their intimist approach to writing.

Magmatic, hallucinatory and alchemical are all useful words to describe the creative process of Herberto Helder, the most intriguing and most influential Portuguese poet after Fernando Pessoa, with whom he seems to bear little resemblance. Pessoa described his own performance as a drama divided into people (the heteronyms) instead of into acts. Helder titled his second book *Poemacto* [Poemact], and it is a song of the self, but a far larger self than the narrator of Florbela Espanca's sonnets. Rather than self-dividing into alter egos like Pessoa, Helder, as a poet, is a continuously exploding I, and his entire output a never-ending poem-act. Maybe he is a throwback to Romanticism — not to the likes of Wordsworth and Keats but to poet-visionaries such as Blake and Hölderlin. His poetry, like the personal universe it ravenously explores, is all passion and transmutation, which to him are practically synonyms.

Herberto Helder folds the outer world into his metamorphic, darkly glowing poetry. Ruy Belo, on the contrary, seems to stretch out his poetic self across space and time, an expansiveness mirrored in his preference for rhythmically unemphatic lines that eschew punctuation, as if imitating gently rolling plains. In "Pilgrim and Guest on Planet Earth", the narrator's home is wherever he happens to be, and his friends "are the most recent ones", whom he hardly even knows. His home is everywhere, and nowhere. This attitude is reminiscent of Álvaro de Campos's desire to be everywhere and everyone, to possess the whole universe, but whereas the desire of Pessoa's heteronym is a "boundless rage" for an all-encompassing sensation (p. 19), Belo's narrator is motivated by a quietly insistent urge to be united to the rest of the world. Belo was a devout Roman Catholic who lost his faith, and much of his poetry chronicles and grapples with the transitory nature of human life, or even a dog's life ("Requiem for a Dog").

The "animal intelligence" idealized by António Ramos Rosa becomes a topic of awed inquiry in the verses of Fiama Hasse Pais Brandão, who begins one of the poems published here with the following admission of envy, or frustration: "I write like an animal, but with less / hallucinatory perfection." Her inquiry proceeds, like the forms of life it engages, with steady persistence: wrapping around, scratching, pecking, penetrating like a mole, and occasionally opening like a flower. Sometimes she is a philosopher writing a Logic of Natural Things. Sometimes she is a disoriented psalmist, in relentless pursuit of the principle or origin responsible for the life her song exalts.

In Luiza Neto Jorge's "Magnolia", it is not the vision of the tree but the swelling sound of the word physically rolling off her tongue that stirs and startles the poet like lightning. Speech, and poetry, are intimately related to the body, which for Jorge is always an erotic body. Her "Houses" personify experiences, attitudes and responses of female sexuality, and in "The House of the World", a minuscule birthmark contains oceans and mountains of sensuality, all music, and the charged history of human relations going back at least to the Greeks and Romans. Single words such as "magnolia", "birthmark" and many others in her poetry, when read slowly, throb with a hidden enormity of feeling and meaning.

Like the four poets discussed in the previous four paragraphs, Vasco Graça Moura published his first collection of verse in the early 1960s, but he did not come fully into his own as a poet until around 1980, and while his work has a highly personal side, marked by autobiographical anecdote (as in the poem "fanny"), I would not call it intimist. He was a multifaceted writer and especially proud of his poetic achievement — which included brilliant translations of Dante's *Divina Commedia* and Shakespeare's sonnets into Portuguese — but he was also deeply committed to public life, sometimes holding political office and heading up cultural projects and institutions. His manner of embracing life in its totality comes through in his poetry, which is about love, history, modernity and cultural issues. He deftly wielded formal kinds of verse but was equally fond of a conversational plain style, which was perhaps the best medium for showing off his intellectual verve, wit, and discernment.

The 1970s and beyond

António Franco Alexandre's poetic style and subject matter have changed dramatically from book to book, and each one is a stunning performance. Since each of his collections creates a new world, which the reader better appreciates by spending a little time there, the six poems translated for this anthology are all taken from a single collection: *Dwelling Places I & II*. The atmospheres generated by these poems are pristine, primitive, sometimes biblical. "I note / the exact emotion of the inexact curve," says the narrator about birds in flight (p. 175), and this describes well the central thrust of his vocation: to precisely record what is imprecise or hard to grasp. In another poem, someone offers the poet the following advice: "don't choose words for themselves / but for how they stand at corners" (p. 171). Meaning resides less in individual words than in the edifice they form, but these poems are not the step-by-step, laboriously built houses that Alberto Caeiro inveighed against. They are strange dwellings, and it is better to roam though them and linger a while, without attempting to interpret too much.

Al Berto brought sex, drugs and rock-and-roll to Portuguese poetry, insofar as his writing was partly inspired by a lifestyle that experienced and experimented without boundaries. He calmed down as he got older, at least on the outside, but he remained a wanderer at heart, and was attracted to the shadowy dark underside of life as well as to sunlit exteriors. He told an interviewer that contact with sordidness helped him, by way of contrast, to understand beauty. His poetry is predominantly narrative and obliquely autobiographical, but not confessional. The sequence of poems translated here as "Salt Spray" is about sailing, desire, fear and sex, all of which are metaphors or motivations for Al Berto's writing.

The seven translations of poems by Nuno Júdice are taken from a single collection, *Meditation on Ruins*, whose title seems to promise something neo-Romantic, and the poet delivers on the promise, but this is Romanticism in a modern mode, or, to put it another way, Romanticism itself is in ruins. The narrator still wants to be a visionary, but he doubts what he sees. Rather than Wordsworth's "emotion recollected in tranquillity", we are given unsettling observations in search of a coherent emotion. An awareness of the world's fundamental chaos was part of the Romantic ethos, and it was up to the poetic ego to in a certain way transcend, without denying, the disparities. But Júdice's poetic I, having fun with the poem in which Álvaro de Campos is served up a dish of cold tripe instead of the warm things like love that life might have given him ("Oporto-style Tripe", p. 23), is served up a dish of himself, "a distant sensation" he finds "cold and tasteless" ("The Last Supper"). The world, meanwhile, is not after all so chaotic; it has a natural order, which humans are helpless to grasp or change ("Pasture").

Poetry, for Ana Luísa Amaral, is part of a balancing act that also involves her life as a woman and mother and her commitment to loving, understood both as amorous devotion and as solidarity with those people or groups of people she feels connected to. I don't mean that she needs her daily life and her experience of loving as thematic material for her poetry, though she does indeed make use of them, but that she could not conceive of writing poems as an isolated act, apart from everything else. The notion of perfect or pure poetry would make no sense to her. Considering it philosophically, she might agree with the Caeiro dictum that "Nature is parts without a whole", but this causes her no angst, and she is not drawn, like Breyner, or like a certain corner of Pessoa's being, to the unity promised by the spiritual dimension. It is the secular human experience — biology, history, culture, language, passion — that demands her full attention. The ideal work of art would be a lived *Victory of Samothrace*, made of flesh and words and a constant readiness to fly.

Amaral's poetry contains frequent allusions to literary predecessors as well as to art works. Adília Lopes, even more literarily allusive, often resorts to parody, particularly of the poets she most admires, and she can promiscuously incorporate other writers' words into her own works, or complete what someone else left unfinished. Aware of themselves as women poets in a field that has long been dominated by men, Amaral and Lopes do not aspire to reconfiguring the poetic canon, but they want to open up a space in contemporary poetry — beginning with their own poems — for specifically female concerns and for a female way of being. Florbela Espanca had to fight just to be recognized as a valid poet in what was virtually an all-male club, and when she passionately wrote about wanting to get lost in love ("To Love!", p. 37), it was not as a helpless woman without other horizons who necessarily depended on men; she was a self-confident lover, rejecting the reputedly female dream of a life built around a monogamous relationship. In Lopes's take-off on Espanca's sonnet, the narrator, who has no love relationships nor even any casual sex, flaunts her fragility and defends her right to be sad not because of love's difficulties and frustrations (a common enough theme in Espanca) but because love is not even a part of her life, except as an impossible dream. Lopes's poem ("I want to fuck to fuck") also comments on the hypocrisy of revolutions that change laws and perceptions but not the power-based nature of human relationships, and it updates, urbanizes and ridicules Fernando Pessoa's idyllic view of a reaper who blithely sings while she works in the field (in Pessoa's poem titled "A Ceifeira" [The Reaper], not included here). Lopes has anointed herself a new and very different Florbela Espanca, without sex appeal or self-exaltation. Her poetry is part of the syllabus for feminist studies, and rightly so. But even more radically she is a poet of the lonely, the pathetic, the banal, and the unpretty. "God is the cleaning woman", affirms one of her poems (not included here).

The "small and useless suicidal / marvel called Europe" is a recurring topic in the poetry of Paulo Teixeira. He attributes that pithy description of a decadent Old World to Stefan Zweig, in the poem "Die Welt von Gestern", which is a kind of versified distillation of the autobiography completed by the Austrian writer the day before he and his second wife committed suicide in Brazil, where they were exiles from Nazi Germany. But Europe is just a symbol, the most immediate and obvious instance, of civilizational decline. The 813 siege of Baghdad is the backdrop for another poem featuring two lovers in a dying world — in this case two unidentified men, given over to each other's body and with desire as their only "genealogical tree". The narrator admits that the nearness of death, raging on the streets of the besieged city, is a "fascinating presence", and the imminent eternity predicted in the final verse seems to signify both the consummation of love and the arrival of death. Time and again, an awareness of life's tenuousness leads to the conclusion that only tender encounters are worth living for. Or is it that love itself seeks a symbolic transfiguration and immortalization in death, which obliterates distance? The poem "Auto-da-fé", on the other hand, posits the sacrificial death of poetry as the necessary condition for love. The word, like the world, is too little.

The poetic sensibility of José Tolentino Mendonça is in some ways the opposite to Teixeira's. Mendonça has this faith: "From land to land all of them connected / we're something that God touches" (from the poem "Strange Eyes"). Revelations are everywhere, even if we don't understand what they mean. And love can exist in a simple gaze exchanged with a stranger ("Calle Príncipe, 25"). The origins of Mendonça's faith — telluric and shakeable, like a seismic country — are described in "The Childhood of Herberto Helder", which is really about his own childhood. (Both poets were born on the island of Madeira.) If back then he found God in the vast skies and the empty wastes, now he finds the Deity in the minutiae of daily life. An admirer of Marianne Moore's predilection for acute observations of the mundane, he playfully "completes" her poetry with suggestions of an underlying (or interlinear) interest in metaphysics and some imaginary biographical details ("The Complete Poetry of Marianne Moore"). At the beginning of this Introduction I cited a poem by João Cabral de Melo Neto that praises Moore — a "crutch poet" — for patiently, capably building her own poetic house. Mendonça's poem reminds us that poetic house-building, whether or not the builders use crutches, is ultimately a community effort, which also includes the readers.

Luís Quintais both admires and actively emulates the work of another American Modernist, Wallace Stevens (1879-1955). The complex relationship between language, objective reality, consciousness and the imagination forms the crux of the Portuguese poet's investigations. Well aware that language and the human mind can represent but never fully apprehend the real world, he points out — in the poem "On Ice" — that the Freudian concept of the unconscious, useful as it is for explaining human psychology and even artistic creativity, is a recent product of evolution, which is the driving force of life as we know it and staunchly impervious to explanation. Nor can he be satisfied by philosophical contemplations and poetry's supreme fictions. In "The World as Representation", after initially wondering about the relationship of his mental image of a dog's howling to the dog's actual howling, the poem's narrator and would-be disciple of Schopenhauer flings open the window, in search of the "preternatural dog" that exists in the dark night beyond his seeing. Real life matters for Quintais, whose "For Animals" forces us to re-examine our thinking about who has the right to take life away, and from whom, and by what means.

I hope that my brief reflections on the poets included in this anthology will help the patient reader to better appreciate their artistic singularity. This should be evident from the poems themselves, but the selections, I'm afraid, are a bit skimpy. In the case of Daniel Faria, however, just two or three poems would be enough to make even a distracted reader realize that something quite different is going on. The poet is on fire — not in the flames of poetry, like Herberto Helder (a crucial influence on Faria), but in the invisible flames of spirit. "I listen without knowing / If what I hear is silence / Or god" remarks Sophia de Mello Breyner in one of her poems (p. 57). Faria is completely given over to that silence, or God, and the poems he writes are the fruits of his attentive listening. "Close listening fills us with juice like a well in a courtyard" (p. 253). He is waiting to die so as to join up with the voice he hears, the silence that talks to him, and while waiting he reports on his soul's journey, exhorting us to imagine what he knows so well by faith. However sceptical we may be, we are disarmed by "The Cycles of Bad Weather", a poetic sequence in which he directly addresses us, pulls us in, takes our hand, exposes his and our fragility, and makes us glimpse with him the mystery of our common life, hypostatized in a magnolia tree, whose real presence (according to Faria) distinguishes it from the "pronounced" magnolia of Luiza Neto Jorge.

"The accuracy of the vernacular!" Marianne Moore once exclaimed in an interview, and we find that accuracy in the colloquially precise diction of the four free-verse poems by Margarida Vale de Gato translated here. This poet, who also makes frequent use of rhyme and traditional forms such as the sonnet, is attentive to the limitations and pitfalls of language ("The Romantic Image") as well as to ethical issues facing the writer. Her "Medea" is not about the original mythological story but about how it is reworked (including in the self-same poem, which changes a few details) and about how writers manipulate the feelings of readers, or spectators, making us sympathize with a mother who murders her children. The writer mentioned in the poem, not incidentally, is male, a detail that makes me think of another poem (not included here), in which Gato has Anna Karenina chiding Tolstoy for not having adequately understood her. A number of her poems enact the styles and sensibilities of women writers, with Emily Dickinson, Virginia Woolf, Sylvia Plath and Christina Rossetti being brought in either as narrators or characters.

Like Gato, Daniel Jonas alternates between formal and free verse. Two of his six collections to date consist of sonnets; the free-verse style of his other collections takes many different shapes, while continuing to be marked by taut syntax. The poems from all his books are conceptually taut, and occasionally demanding on the reader. Their mood is frequently nostalgic, and part of that nostalgia may be for a different poetic milieu, since Jonas's work seems a little out of place in 21st-century Portugal. It would be equally out of place in earlier periods. Although firmly rooted in tradition (in the Eliotian sense), its roots extend far and wide. That said, the inspiration for his poem "Houses" is actually quite close to home (pun not intended, but welcome), since Portuguese poetry is a little obsessed by houses. For Luiza Neto Jorge they represent various attitudes of the erotic body (pp. 149–153). For Ruy Belo (p. 131) they have to do with stability and the need to belong. In Herberto Helder, whose "Preface" (p. 115) decisively put houses on Portugal's poetic map, they stand for various things, but mostly for poetry itself. Jonas's narrator dreams of living inside all of these houses but is deathly afraid of being trapped — whether that trap is a finite body, the feeling of definitively belonging somewhere, or a particular poetic trend, a particular poetic style. He visits houses for brief moments only, and flies onward, and sometimes backwards.

The abundance of literal and metaphorical houses in Portuguese poetry after Pessoa (this anthology could have included a number of other "house poems") may be connected to the fact that many poets spent long periods abroad or at any rate felt alienated from their nation when it was ruled by an authoritarian government in which they had no voice. Or it could be a reaction to the Portuguese imperative to travel and emigrate that goes back to the Age of Discovery, when seamen and colonists were recruited in large numbers. "Sad the man who lives at home, / Content with his hearth," decreed Pessoa in a poem from *Mensagem* [*Message*] that exhorted his countrymen to keep going abroad, imaginatively if not physically. (And many of them had to go abroad, for political or economic reasons.)

Although harshly critical of Portugal's governing class and ambivalent about its colonial empire, Pessoa was proud of its maritime achievements, and the same can be said for Sophia de Mello Breyner, whose dozen or so poetry collections include one titled *Navegações* [Navigations]. But other poets converted the theme of voyage into a trope for very different kinds of discoveries, particularly sexual ones. In Breyner's "Beach", pine trees are nostalgic for the old days when they were used as masts for the navigators' ships. But in Mário Cesariny's "The ship of mirrors" (third stanza from the end) and even more obviously in the fourth stanza of the Al Berto selection presented here, the masts are phallic objects of homoerotic desire. Eugénio de Andrade's "Voyage" is also about homoerotic attraction, or its aftermath, and homoeroticism shows up as well in poems by Paulo Teixeira ("During the Siege of Baghdad, 813"), by António Franco Alexandre (in poems not published here, except perhaps the last one in the group), and by older poets, including Fernando Pessoa. Women poets in this anthology, as already demonstrated, have asserted their right to be writers on a par with men, to be women who are not like men, and to be erotic women, whether or not men find them erotically appealing. These various affirmations of sexual freedom and this questioning of traditional sexual roles and attitudes occurred without marches or conspicuous movements to raise consciousness and challenge preconceptions. Such movements would have been hard to organize and promote before the democratic revolution of 1974. Or perhaps not so hard, according to a poet such as Alexandre O'Neill, critical of Portugal's ruling oligarchy but even more critical of the people's seemingly endemic passivity. The nation's poets, at least in their writing, have been comparatively courageous.

Most of the poets in this anthology would not disagree with W. H. Auden's observation that "poetry makes nothing happen", but Portuguese poetry throughout the 20th century and into the 21st has been a dynamic, wide-open territory, whose inhabitants have spoken with candour and been restlessly inventive, using language to embody their different sexualities, political and cultural preoccupations, amorous passions, religious passions, and in some cases just their yearning for solitude, or the pioneer's yen to pick up and move on, without really knowing to what end. Poetry makes nothing happen, but Auden also observed that it survives "in the valley of its making" and is itself a "way of happening".

About the selection and translations

The modest title of this anthology was chosen to reflect the modesty of its scope. It embraces a number of Portuguese poets whose work I admire. The subjectivity of my selection becomes especially flagrant towards the end of the book, since there are many other youngish Portuguese poets ("youngish" here means at least forty years old) I might have included. An arbiter who relies largely on personal taste and aesthetic affinity must admit the somewhat arbitrary nature of his decisions. Few scholars and critics of Portuguese poetry would take issue with most of the names I have included on my list, but they would all feel that one or another poet was wrongly excluded. Another problem with anthologies like this one is the limited number of pages allotted to each poet. I referred above to the "artistic singularity" of the poets translated and published here. That singularity is usually composed of multiple facets, which cannot be adequately represented by four or five poems. On the plus side, an anthology can highlight the crisscrossing echoes and influences — as well as the variety and disparities — within a certain linguistic space over a given time period. But again, only some of those echoes and influences have made it into this anthology.

The idea for an anthology of Portuguese poetry in English translation originated with Bernardo Futscher Pereira, who met with me in 2012, shortly before taking up his post as Portugal's ambassador to Ireland. I said fine, provided you can find an interested publisher. Dedalus Press was very interested, we discussed the general contours and characteristics of the anthology, and I asked Alexis Levitin if he would contribute some of his many excellent translations. He kindly agreed and would have been willing to translate work by other poets on my list, but I had most of them covered, and the time was short, so a large majority of the translations are my own. Here is a list of Levitin's translations published here:

- Jorge de Sena: all except "Sigefried's Funeral March";
- Carlos de Oliveira: the entire section;
- Eugénio de Andrade: the entire section;
- Alexandre O'Neill (1924-1986): "The History of Morality", "Turkey", and "First Serious Warning";
- Fiama Hasse Pais Brandão: all except "Song of Places" and "Song of Genesis".

Many of Levitin's and my translations have been previously published, but we have carefully re-examined and often revised them for this publication. Both of us are grateful to our Portuguese friends who helped clarify assorted doubts. Pat Boran and Bernardo Futscher Pereira closely read the final manuscript and made a number of helpful suggestions. Additional translations of work from poets in this anthology as well as from many other Portuguese poets can be found on two internet sites: "Poetry International Rotterdam" and "Poems from the Portuguese".

My appreciation of Portuguese poetry, and parts of my Introduction, owe debts to a number of critics, some of whom are themselves notable poets: Cláudia Pazos Alonso, Fernando Pinto do Amaral, João Barrento, Gastão Cruz, António Guerreiro, Fernando Guimarães, Manuel Gusmão, Anna M. Klobucka, Oscar Lopes, Joaquim Manuel Magalhães, Rosa Maria Martelo, Fernando Cabral Martins, Pedro Mexia, Eduardo Pitta, Luís

Miguel Queirós and Osvaldo Manuel Silvestre. There are other fine critics, but these are the ones (the ones I happen to remember!) who have illuminated my understanding of poets in this volume, excluding Pessoa, for whom the list of critics would be too long.

Thanks are also due to the poets — or the poets' heirs — and their publishers for allowing their work to be included in this volume.

Richard Zenith
Lisbon, June 2014

from O GUARDADOR DE REBANHOS

I

Eu nunca guardei rebanhos,
Mas é como se os guardasse.
Minha alma é como um pastor,
Conhece o vento e o sol
E anda pela mão das Estações
A seguir e a olhar.
Toda a paz da Natureza sem gente
Vem sentar-se a meu lado.
Mas eu fico triste como um pôr de sol
Para a nossa imaginação,
Quando esfria no fundo da planície
E se sente a noite entrada
Como uma borboleta pela janela.

Alberto Caeiro

1889–1915. Born in Lisbon, where he also died, from tuberculosis, but spent most of his life in the Ribatejo countryside, north and east of Lisbon. Had little formal education and no real profession, but the small inheritance left by his parents adequately covered his modest expenses. Lived for at least part of the time with a great-aunt. Was in contact with Ricardo Reis, Álvaro de Campos and Fernando Pessoa, all of whom considered him to be their poetic master.

---

from THE KEEPER OF SHEEP

I

I've never kept sheep,
But it's as if I kept them.
My soul is like a shepherd.
It knows the wind and sun,
And walks hand in hand with the Seasons
Looking at what passes.
All the peace of Nature without people
Sits down by my side.
But I get sad like a sunset
In our imagination
When the cold drifts over the plain
And we feel the night come in
Like a butterfly through the window.

Mas a minha tristeza é sossego
Porque é natural e justa
E é o que deve estar na alma
Quando já pensa que existe
E as mãos colhem flores sem ela dar por isso.

Como um ruído de chocalhos
Para além da curva da estrada,
Os meus pensamentos são contentes.
Só tenho pena de saber que eles são contentes,
Porque, se o não soubesse,
Em vez de serem contentes e tristes,
Seriam alegres e contentes.

Pensar incomoda como andar à chuva
Quando o vento cresce e parece que chove mais.

Não tenho ambições nem desejos.
Ser poeta não é uma ambição minha.
É a minha maneira de estar sozinho.

E se desejo às vezes,
Por imaginar, ser cordeirinho
(Ou ser o rebanho todo
Para andar espalhado por toda a encosta
A ser muita cousa feliz ao mesmo tempo),
É só porque sinto o que escrevo ao pôr do sol,
Ou quando uma nuvem passa a mão por cima da luz
E corre um silêncio pela erva fora.

Quando me sento a escrever versos
Ou, passeando pelos caminhos ou pelos atalhos,
Escrevo versos num papel que está no meu pensamento,
Sinto um cajado nas mãos
E vejo um recorte de mim
No cimo dum outeiro,
Olhando para o meu rebanho e vendo as minhas ideias
Ou olhando para as minhas ideias e vendo o meu rebanho,

Yet my sadness is a comfort
For it is natural and right
And is what should fill the soul
Whenever it thinks it exists
And doesn't notice the hands that pick flowers.

Like a sound of sheep-bells
Beyond the bend in the road
My thoughts are content.
My only regret is that I know they're content,
Since if I did not know it
They would be content and happy
Instead of sadly content.

Thinking is a discomfort, like walking in the rain
When the wind kicks up and it seems to rain harder.

I have no ambitions and no desires.
To be a poet is not my ambition,
It's my way of being alone.

And if sometimes, in my imagination,
I desire to be a small lamb
(Or to be the whole flock
So that I can roam all over the hillside
As many happy things at the same time),
It's only because I feel what I write when the sun sets
Or when a cloud passes its hand over the light
And a silence sweeps through the grass.

When I sit down to write verses
Or I walk along roads and pathways
Jotting verses on a piece of paper in my mind,
I feel a staff in my hand
And see my own profile
On top of a low hill
Looking after my flock and seeing my ideas,
Or looking after my ideas and seeing my flock,

E sorrindo vagamente como quem não compreende o que se diz
E quer fingir que compreende.

Saúdo todos os que me lerem,
Tirando-lhes o chapéu largo
Quando me vêem à minha porta
Mal a diligência levanta no cimo do outeiro.
Saúdo-os e desejo-lhes sol,
E chuva, quando a chuva é precisa,
E que as suas casas tenham
Ao pé duma janela aberta
Uma cadeira predilecta
Onde se sentem, lendo os meus versos.
E ao lerem os meus versos pensem
Que sou qualquer cousa natural —
Por exemplo, a árvore antiga
À sombra da qual quando crianças
Se sentavam com um baque, cansados de brincar,
E limpavam o suor da testa quente
Com a manga do bibe riscado.

X

«Olá, guardador de rebanhos,
Aí à beira da estrada,
Que te diz o vento que passa?»

«Que é vento, e que passa,
E que já passou antes,
E que passará depois.
E a ti o que te diz?»

«Muita cousa mais do que isso.
Fala-me de muitas outras cousas.
De memórias e de saudades
E de cousas que nunca foram.»

And smiling vaguely, like one who doesn't grasp what was said
But pretends he did.

I salute all who may read me,
Tipping my wide-brimmed hat
As soon as the coach tops the hill
And they see me at my door.
I salute them and wish them sunshine,
Or rain, if rain is needed,
And a favourite chair where they sit
At home, reading my poems
Next to an open window.
And as they read my poems, I hope
They think I'm something natural —
That old tree, for instance,
In whose shade when they were children
They sat down with a thud, tired of playing,
And wiped the sweat from their hot foreheads
With the sleeve of their striped smocks.

X

"Hello, keeper of sheep
There on the side of the road.
What does the blowing wind say to you?"

"That it's wind and it blows,
That it has blown before,
And that it will blow hereafter.
And what does it say to you?"

"Much more than that.
It speaks to me of many other things.
Of memories and longings,
And of things that never were."

«Nunca ouviste passar o vento.
O vento só fala do vento.
O que lhe ouviste foi mentira,
E a mentira está em ti.»

XXIII

O meu olhar azul como o céu
É calmo como a água ao sol.
É assim, azul e calmo,
Porque não interroga nem se espanta…

Se eu interrogasse e me espantasse
Não nasciam flores novas nos prados
Nem mudaria qualquer cousa no sol de modo a ele ficar mais
belo.
(Mesmo se nascessem flores novas no prado
E se o sol mudasse para mais belo,
Eu sentiria menos flores no prado
E achava mais feio o sol…
Porque tudo é como é e assim é que é,
E eu aceito, e nem agradeço,
Para não parecer que penso nisso…)

XXXVIII

Bendito seja o mesmo sol de outras terras
Que faz meus irmãos todos os homens,
Porque todos os homens, um momento no dia, o olham como eu,
E nesse puro momento
Todo limpo e sensível
Regressam imperfeitamente
E com um suspiro que mal sentem
Ao Homem verdadeiro e primitivo
Que via o sol nascer e ainda o não adorava.
Porque isso é natural — mais natural
Que adorar o sol e depois Deus
E depois tudo o mais que não há.

"You've never heard the wind blow.
The wind only speaks of the wind.
What you heard was a lie,
And the lie is in you."

XXIII

My gaze, blue like the sky,
Is calm like water in the sunlight.
It is blue and calm
Because it does not question or stare in astonishment.

If I questioned and were astonished,
New flowers would not sprout in the meadows
Nor would anything change in the sun to make it more
beautiful.
(Even if new flowers sprouted in the meadow
And the sun changed to become more beautiful,
I would feel fewer flowers in the meadow
And find less beauty in the sun.
Because everything is what it is, which is how it should be,
And I accept it, and don't even give thanks,
Since that might suggest I think about it.)

XXXVIII

Blessed be the same sun of other lands
For making all men my brothers
Since all men, at some moment in the day, look at it as I do.
And in that pure, limpid
And sensitive moment
They partially return
With a sigh they hardly feel
To the true and primitive Man
Who saw the sun come up and did not yet worship it.
For this is what is natural — more natural
Than worshiping the sun, then God,
And then everything else that doesn't exist.

from ODES

BOCAS ROXAS de vinho,
Testas brancas sob rosas,
Nus, brancos antebraços
Deixados sobre a mesa:

Tal seja, Lídia, o quadro
Em que fiquemos, mudos,
Eternamente inscritos
Na consciência dos deuses.

Antes isto que a vida
Como os homens a vivem,
Cheia da negra poeira
Que erguem das estradas.

Ricardo Reis

Born in 1887, in Oporto. Attended a Jesuit high school and then earned a medical degree. Politically a royalist (his last name means “kings”), immigrated to Brazil in 1919, after a monarchist coup in northern Portugal was successfully put down by the republicans, who had come to power in 1910. Reis was at a certain point based in Peru, and he also taught Latin in an American high school, but his ultimate fate is a mystery. Author of Horatian-style odes and also of unfinished prose works, including a preface to the poetry of Alberto Caeiro. Proponent of “neo-paganism”, a doctrine elucidated in his prose and reflected in his odes.

---

from ODES

LIPS RED from wine,
White brows beneath roses,
Naked white forearms
Lying on the table:

May this be the picture
Wherein speechless, Lydia,
We’ll forever be inscribed
In the minds of the gods.

Rather this than life
As earthly men live it,
Full of the black dust
They raise from the roads.

Só os deuses socorrem
Com seu exemplo aqueles
Que nada mais pretendem
Que ir no rio das cousas.

PREFIRO ROSAS, meu amor, à pátria,
    E antes magnólias amo
    Que fama e que virtude.
Logo que a vida me não canse, deixo
    Que a vida por mim passe
    Logo que eu fique o mesmo.
Que importa àquele a quem já nada importa
    Que um perca e outro vença,
    Se a aurora raia sempre,
Se cada ano com a primavera
    Aparecem as folhas
    E com o outono cessam?
E o resto, as outras cousas que os humanos
    Acrescentam à vida,
    Que me aumentam na alma?
Nada, salvo o desejo de indif'rença
    E a confiança mole
    Na hora fugitiva.

SE RECORDO quem fui, outrem me vejo,
E o passado é um presente na lembrança.
    Quem fui é alguém que amo
    Porém somente em sonho.
E a saudade que me aflige a mente
Não é de mim nem do passado visto,
    Senão de quem habito
    Por trás dos olhos cegos.

The gods, by their example,
Help only those
Who seek to go nowhere
But in the river of things.

I PREFER ROSES, my love, to the homeland,
  And I love magnolias
  Over fame and virtue.
As long as this passing life does not weary
  Or change who I am,
  Let it keep passing.
What does it matter who wins or loses
  If nothing matters to me
  And the dawn still breaks,
And each year with spring the leaves appear,
  And each year with autumn
  They fall from the trees?
What does all the rest, the things that humans
  Add on to life,
  Increase in my soul?
Nothing, except its desire for indifference
  And its languid trust
  In the fleeting moment.

LOOKING BACK, I see a different me,
And the past is a present in memory.
  Who I was is someone
  I love, but only in a dream.
My mind is tormented by nostalgia
Not for me or the reseen past
  But for the one I inhabit
  Behind my unseeing eyes.

Nada, senão o instante, me conhece.
Minha mesma lembrança é nada, e sinto
        Que quem sou e quem fui
        São sonhos diferentes.

PONHO NA ALTIVA MENTE o fixo esforço
        Da altura, e à sorte deixo,
        E a suas leis, o verso;
Que, quando é alto e régio o pensamento,
        Súbdita a frase o busca
        E o 'scravo ritmo o serve.

EU NUNCA FUI DOS que a um sexo o outro
No amor ou na amizade preferiram.
Por igual a beleza eu apeteço
        Seja onde for, beleza.
Pousa a ave, olhando apenas a que pousa,
Pondo querer pousar antes do ramo;
Corre o rio onde encontra o seu declive
        E não onde é preciso.
Assim das diferenças me separo
E onde amo, porque o amor me calhou, amo.
Nem a inocência inata quando se ama
        Julgo postergada nisto.
Não no objecto, no modo está o amor.
Logo que a ame, a qualquer cousa amo.
Meu amor nela não reside, mas
        Em meu amor.
Os deuses que nos deram este rumo
Do amor a que chamamos a beleza
Não na mulher só a puseram; nem
        No fruto apenas.

Nothing, except the moment, knows me.
My very memory is nothing. Who
    I am and who I was
    I feel as different dreams.

I DEVOTE MY HIGHER MIND to the ardent
    Pursuit of the summit, leaving
    Verse to chance and its laws,
For when the thought is lofty and noble,
    The sentence will naturally seek it,
    And rhythm slavishly serve it.

I WAS NEVER ONE who in love or in friendship
Preferred one sex over the other. Beauty
Attracts me in equal measure wherever
    I find it, beauty.
The bird alights, looking only to its alighting,
Its desire to alight mattering more than the branch.
The river runs where it finds its slope,
    And not where it is needed.
Thus I separate myself from distinctions
And love where I love, because love happened,
And I don't offend the inherent innocence
    Of the act of loving.
Love is not in the object but the manner.
I love something only when I start loving it.
My love does not reside in it
    But in my love.
The gods who gave us this path
Of love that we call beauty
Did not place it only in women
    Or only in fruit.

Também deram a flor p'ra que a colhéssemos
E com melhor amor talvez colhamos
        O que pra usar buscamos.

SOLENE PASSA SOBRE a fértil terra
A branca, inútil nuvem fugidia,
Que um negro instante de entre os campos ergue
        Um sopro arrefecido.
Tal me alta na alma a lenta ideia voa
E me enegrece a mente, mas já torno,
Como a si mesmo o mesmo campo, ao dia
        Superfície da vida.

VIVEM EM NÓS inúmeros;
Se penso ou sinto, ignoro
Quem é que pensa ou sente.
Sou somente o lugar
Onde se sente ou pensa.

Tenho mais almas que uma.
Há mais eus do que eu mesmo.
Existo todavia
Indiferente a todos.
Faço-os calar: eu falo.

Os impulsos cruzados
Do que sinto ou não sinto
Disputam em quem sou.
Ignoro-os. Nada dictam
A quem me sei: eu escrevo.

They also gave us the flower to pluck.
And perhaps we pluck with better love
        What we seek for the using.

SOLEMNLY OVER the fertile land
The brief and futile white cloud passes,
And for a black instant the fields are touched
        By a cold breeze.
So too in my soul the slow thought soars
And darkens my mind, but I, like the field
That returns to itself, return to the day,
        The surface of life.

COUNTLESS LIVES inhabit us.
I don't know, when I think or feel,
Who is thinking or feeling.
I am merely the place
Where things are thought or felt.

I have more than one soul.
There are more I's than I myself.
I exist, nevertheless,
Indifferent to them all.
I silence them: I speak.

The crossing urges of what
I feel or do not feel
Struggle in who I am, but I
Ignore them. They dictate nothing
To the I I know: I write.

UMA VONTADE FÍSICA de comer o universo
Toma às vezes o lugar do meu pensamento...
Uma fúria desmedida
A conquistar a posse como que absorvedora
Dos céus e das estrelas
Persegue-me como um remorso de não ter cometido um crime.

Como quem olha um mar
Olho os que partem em viagem...
Olho os comboios como quem os estranha,
Grandes cousas férreas e absurdas que levam almas,
Que levam consciências da vida e de si próprias
Para lugares verdadeiramente reais,
Para os lugares que — custa a crer — realmente existem
Não sei como, mas é no espaço e no tempo
E têm gente que tem vidas reais
Seguidas hora a hora como as nossas vidas...

Álvaro de Campos

Born in 1890, in Tavira, the Algarve. Studied engineering in Scotland, first mechanical and then naval. Made a voyage to the Far East and then worked for a number of years in England, as a naval engineer. Spent long periods in Lisbon, where he settled down in the late 1920s, at which point he quit working. Gave interviews and contributed opinion pieces to periodicals, sometimes disagreeing with the opinions expressed by Fernando Pessoa. Author of a vast body of poetry and of numerous prose works. His "Notes for the Memory of my Master Caeiro" narrate some of the meetings that took place between him, Caeiro, Reis, Pessoa and António Mora, a philosopher.

A PHYSICAL URGE to eat the universe
Sometimes takes the place of my thought.
A boundless rage
Craving to possess, as if by absorption,
All the skies and stars
Hounds me like a regret for a crime not committed.

I look at the departing passengers
As if I were looking at an ocean.
I look at the trains as if at strange objects,
Absurd iron contraptions that transport souls,
Each one a consciousness of life and of itself,
To genuinely real places,
To places that — hard to believe — really exist
In space and time, though I don't know how,
And they're inhabited by people with real lives
Lived, like our lives, hour after hour.

Ah, por uma nova sensação física
Pela qual eu possuísse o universo inteiro,
Um novo tacto que fizesse pertencer-me,
A meu ser possuidor fisicamente,
O universo com todos os seus sóis e as suas estrelas
E as vidas múltiplas das suas almas…

ATRAVÉS DO RUÍDO do café cheio de gente
Chega-me a brisa que passa pelo convés
Nas longas viagens, no alto mar, no verão
Perto dos trópicos (no amontoado nocturno do navio —
Sacudido regularmente pela hélice palpitante —
Vejo passar os uniformes brancos dos oficiais de bordo).
E essa brisa traz um ruído de mar-alto, pluro-mar
E a nossa civilização não pertence à minha reminiscência.

OLHA, DAISY: quando eu morrer tu hás-de
Dizer aos meus amigos aí de Londres,
Embora não o sintas, que tu escondes
A grande dor da minha morte. Irás de

Londres p'ra York, onde nasceste (dizes…
Que eu nada que tu digas acredito),
Contar àquele pobre rapazito
Que me deu tantas horas tão felizes,

Embora não o saibas, que morri…
Mesmo ele, a quem eu tanto julguei amar,
Nada se importará… Depois vai dar

Ah, what I'd give for a new physical sensation
That would make the whole universe belong to me,
A new kind of touch by which I
Could possess, physically possess,
The universe with all its suns and its stars
And the multiple lives of its souls!

THROUGH THE NOISE of the café full of people
Comes the breeze that blows over the deck
On long voyages, in the summer at high sea
Near the tropics. (On the nocturnally looming ship
— Steadily shaken by the fluttering propeller —
I see the white uniforms of officers pass by.)
And the breeze brings me a high-sea, multi-sea sound,
And our civilization has no part in this memory.

LISTEN, DAISY. When I die, although
You may not feel a thing, you must
Tell all my friends in London how much
My loss makes you suffer. Then go

To York, where you claim you were born
(But I don't believe a thing you claim),
To tell that poor boy who gave me
So many hours of joy (but of course

You don't know about that) that I'm dead.
Even he, whom I thought I sincerely
Loved, won't care... Then go and break

A notícia a essa estranha Cecily
Que acreditava que eu seria grande…
Raios partam a vida e quem lá ande!

DOBRADA À MODA DO PORTO

Um dia, num restaurante, fora do espaço e do tempo,
Serviram-me o amor como dobrada fria.
Disse delicadamente ao missionário da cozinha
Que a preferia quente,
Que a dobrada (e era à moda do Porto) nunca se come fria.

Impacientaram-se comigo.
Nunca se pode ter razão, nem num restaurante.
Não comi, não pedi outra coisa, paguei a conta,
E vim passear para toda a rua.

Quem sabe o que isto quer dizer?
Eu não sei, e foi comigo…

(Sei muito bem que na infância de toda a gente houve um jardim,
Particular ou público, ou do vizinho.
Sei muito bem que brincarmos era o dono dele.
E que a tristeza é de hoje.)

Sei isso muitas vezes,
Mas, se eu pedi amor, por que é que me trouxeram
Dobrada à moda do Porto fria?
Não é prato que se possa comer frio,
Mas trouxeram-mo frio.
Não me queixei, mas estava frio,
Nunca se pode comer frio, mas veio frio.

The news to that strange girl Cecily,
Who believed that one day I'd be great...
To hell with life and everyone in it!

OPORTO-STYLE TRIPE

One day, in a restaurant, outside of space and time,
I was served up love as a dish of cold tripe.
I politely told the kitchen missionary
That I preferred it hot,
Because tripe (and it was Oporto-style) is never eaten cold.

They got impatient with me.
You can never be right, not even in a restaurant.
I didn't eat it, I ordered nothing else, I paid the bill,
And I decided to take a walk down the street.

Who knows what this might mean?
I don't know, and it happened to me...

(I know very well that in everyone's childhood there was a garden,
Private or public, or belonging to the neighbour.
I know very well that our playing made us its owner
And that sadness belongs to today.)

I know this many times over,
But if I asked for love, why did they bring me
Oporto-style tripe that was cold?
It's not a dish that can be eaten cold,
But they served it to me cold.
I didn't make a fuss, but it was cold.
It can never be eaten cold, but it came cold.

FAZE AS MALAS para Parte Nenhuma!
Embarca para a universalidade negativa de tudo
Com um grande embandeiramento de navios fingidos —
Dos navios pequenos, multicolores, da infância!
Faze as malas para o Grande Abandono!
E não esqueças, entre as escovas e a tesoura,
A distância policroma do que se não pode obter.
Faze as malas definitivamente!
Que és tu aqui, onde existes gregário e inútil —
E quanto mais útil mais inútil —
E quanto mais verdadeiro mais falso —
Que és tu aqui? que és tu aqui? que és tu aqui?
Embarca, sem malas mesmo, para ti mesmo diverso!
Que te é a terra habitada senão o que não é contigo?

COMEÇO A CONHECER-ME. Não existo.
Sou o intervalo entre o que desejo ser e os outros me fizeram,
Ou metade desse intervalo, porque também há vida ...
Sou isso, enfim...
Apague a luz, feche a porta e deixe de ter barulhos de chinelos
no corredor.
Fique eu no quarto só com o grande sossego de mim mesmo.
É um universo barato.

PACK YOUR BAGS for Nowhere at All!
Set sail for the ubiquitous negation of everything
With a panoply of flags on make-believe ships —
Those miniature, multi-coloured ships from childhood!
Pack your bags for the Grand Departure!
And don't forget, along with your brushes and clippers,
The polychrome distance of what can't be had.
Pack your bags once and for all!
Who are you here, where you're gregarious and useless —
And the more useful the more useless,
The more true to life, the less true to yourself?
Who are you here?, who are you here?, who are you here?
Set sail, even without bags, for your own diverse self!
What does the inhabited world have to do with you?

I'M BEGINNING TO KNOW MYSELF. I don't exist.
I'm the gap between what I'd like to be and what others have
made me,
Or half of this gap, since there's also life...
That's me. Period.
Turn off the light, shut the door, and silence that shuffle of slippers
in the hall.
Leave me alone in my room with the vast peace of myself.
It's a shoddy universe.

MAR. MANHÃ.

Suavemente grande avança
Cheia de sol a onda do mar;
Pausadamente se balança,
E desce como a descansar.

Tão lenta e longa que parece
Duma criança de Titã
O glauco seio que adormece,
Arfando à brisa da manhã.

Parece ser um ente apenas
Este correr da onda do mar,
Como uma cobra que em serenas
Dobras se alongue a colear.

Fernando Pessoa

1888–1935. Born in Lisbon. Spent nine years of his childhood in Durban, South Africa, returning to Lisbon at the age of 17. Studied for two years at Lisbon's School of Arts and Letters (later incorporated into the University of Lisbon), without sitting for any exams. Earned his living as a freelance, doing translations and drafting letters in English for firms with business connections abroad. Frequent contributor to periodicals, where he published poems, creative prose, literary criticism and political commentary. Co-editor of several magazines (*Orpheu*, 1915; *Athena*, 1924-25) and founder of a short-lived publishing house (Olisipo, 1921-23). In addition to poetry, wrote prose on an endless variety of topics. Student of world religions and of Western hermetic traditions. Proficient astrologer. Inventor, in 1914, of Alberto Caeiro, Ricardo Reis and Álvaro de Campos.

OCEAN. MORNING.

Gleaming with sunlight, softly
Surging, the wave advances.
It tosses this way and that,
And falls as if relaxing,

So long and slow it seems
Like the sleeping blue-green breast
Of a child of the Titans
Breathing in the morning breeze.

The rolling of an ocean wave
Resembles a living thing:
A snake that slithers forward
With placid turns and twists.

Unido e vasto e interminável
No são sossego azul do sol,
Arfa com um mover-se estável
O oceano ébrio de arrebol.

E a minha sensação é nula,
Quer de prazer, quer de pesar…
Ébria de alheia a mim ondula
Na onda lúcida do mar.

ÀS VEZES SOU O DEUS que trago em mim
E então eu sou o deus, e o crente e a prece
        E a imagem de marfim
        Em que esse deus se esquece.

Às vezes não sou mais do que um ateu
Desse deus meu que eu sou quando me exalto.
        Olho em mim todo um céu
        E é um mero oco céu alto.

COMO INÚTIL taça cheia
Que ninguém ergue da mesa,
Transborda de dor alheia
Meu coração sem tristeza.

Sonhos de mágoa figura
Só para ter que sentir
E assim não tem a amargura
Que se enternece a fingir.

United, vast and unending
In the peaceful solar blue,
The ocean unmovingly pitches,
Drunk on the dusk's red hue.

But my own sensation is devoid
Of pleasure as well as of pain:
Drunk with estrangement from me,
It rocks on the bright ocean wave.

AT TIMES I'M THE GOD that lives in me,
And then I'm the god, the believer, the prayer
    And the image made of ivory
    In which this god disappears.

At times I'm no more than an atheist
Of this god I am when exalted. I see
    An entire sky in myself,
    And it's just a high, blank sky.

LIKE A USELESSLY full glass
Which no one lifts from the table,
My unsad heart overflows
With a sorrow not its own.

It dreams up sorrowful scenes
Just to have to feel them,
And thus is spared the grief
It feigns while sweetly sighing.

Ficção num palco sem tábuas,
Vestida de papel-seda,
Mima uma dança de mágoas
Para que nada suceda.

GUARDO AINDA, como um pasmo
Em que a infância sobrevive,
Metade do entusiasmo
Que tenho porque já tive.

Quase às vezes me envergonho
De crer tanto em que não creio.
É uma espécie de sonho
Com a realidade ao meio.

Girassol do falso agrado,
Em torno do centro mudo
Fala, amarelo, pasmado
Do negro centro que é tudo.

ISTO

Dizem que finjo ou minto
Tudo que escrevo. Não.
Eu simplesmente sinto
Com a imaginação.
Não uso o coração.

Tudo que sonho ou passo,
O que me falha ou finda,
É como que um terraço

Fiction on a stage not of boards,
Dressed up in tissue paper,
It mimics a dance of sorrows
So that nothing ever occurs.

LIKE AN ASTONISHMENT in which
my childhood survives, I still have
half my enthusiasm — mine
because I had it back then.

I sometimes feel embarrassed
To believe so much in what I don't
Believe. It's a kind of dream
With reality in the middle.

Around its silent centre
The sunflower, falsely pleasing,
Speaks, yellow and astonished
By the black centre that's everything.

THIS

They say I lie or feign
In all I write. Not true.
It's simply that I feel
By way of imagination.
The heart I never use.

All I dream or live,
All that fails me or ceases
To be, is like a terrace

Sobre outra cousa ainda.
Essa cousa é que é linda.

Por isso escrevo em meio
Do que não está ao pé,
Livre do meu enleio,
Sério do que não é.
Sentir? Sinta quem lê!

NESTA GRANDE OSCILAÇÃO
Entre crer e mal descrer
Transtorna-se o coração
Cheio de nada saber;

E, alheado do que sabe
Por não saber o que é,
Só um intento lhe cabe,
Que é o conhecer a fé —

A fé, que os astros conhecem
Porque é a aranha que está
Na teia que todos tecem,
E é a vida que neles há.

Above some other thing.
That thing is what's lovely.

That's why I write in the midst
Of whatever isn't near me,
Freed from my reality,
Serious about what isn't.
Feel? That's up to the reader!

THIS GREAT WAVERING between
Believing and not quite dis-
Believing troubles the heart
Weary of knowing nothing.

Estranged from what it knows
For not knowing what it is,
The heart has only one reason
To be, the finding of faith —

The faith that all the stars
Share, for it is the spider
Whose web they weave, and it is
The life that in them shines.

VAIDADE

Sonho que sou a Poetisa eleita,
Aquela que diz tudo e tudo sabe,
Que tem a inspiração pura e perfeita,
Que reúne num verso a imensidade!

Sonho que um verso meu tem claridade
Para encher o mundo! E que deleita
Mesmo aqueles que morrem de saudade!
Mesmo os de alma profunda e insatisfeita!

Sonho que sou Alguém cá neste mundo...
Aquela de saber vasto e profundo,
Aos pés de quem a Terra anda curvada!

E quando mais no céu eu vou sonhando,
E quando mais no alto ando voando,

Florbela Espanca

1894–1930. Born in Vila Viçosa, a town one hundred miles due east of Lisbon. Studied Law at the University of Lisbon (1917-1920), without taking a degree. Frequent contributor of poems and prose pieces to periodicals. Translated novels from the French. Impassioned in life as well as in her writing, she divorced twice and married three times. Subject to depression and nervous disorders, she died on her 36th birthday from what was probably an intentional overdose of barbiturates.

VANITY

I dream I'm the chosen Poetess,
The one who knows and says everything,
Whose inspiration is pure and perfect,
Who in one verse sums up infinity!

I dream that a verse of mine sheds light
Enough to fill the world! And delights
Even those who die of longing! Even
Those with a deep, dissatisfied soul!

I dream I'm Someone in this world…
The one with knowledge vast and deep,
At whose feet the whole Earth bows!

And when I ascend to heaven, dreaming,
And when in the heights I find myself flying,

Acordo do meu sonho...
E não sou nada!...

AMAR!

Eu quero amar, amar perdidamente!
Amar só por amar: Aqui... além...
Mais Este e Aquele, o Outro e toda a gente
Amar! Amar! E não amar ninguém!

Recordar? Esquecer? Indiferente!...
Prender ou desprender? É mal? É bem?
Quem disser que se pode amar alguém
Durante a vida inteira é porque mente!

Há uma Primavera em cada vida:
É preciso cantá-la assim florida,
Pois se Deus nos deu voz, foi pra cantar!

E se um dia hei-de ser pó, cinza e nada
Que seja a minha noite uma alvorada,
Que me saiba perder... pra me encontrar...

RENÚNCIA

A minha mocidade outrora eu pus
No tranqüilo convento da Tristeza;
Lá passa dias, noites, sempre presa,
Olhos fechados, magras mãos em cruz...

I wake up from my dream…
And I'm nothing! ...

TO LOVE!

I want to love, to be lost in love!
To love just to love: Here... there...
This one, that one, another one,
Everyone! To love and not love anyone!

Remember? Forget? It's all the same!...
Hold on or let go? Wrong? Or right?
Those who say they can love someone
Their whole life long are telling a lie!

There is in every life a Spring.
When it flowers, it must be sung.
The voice God gave us is for singing!

If I must come to ashes, dust,
Nothing, then let my night be a dawn
And let me be lost... to find myself...

RENUNCIATION

Long ago I placed my youth
In the quiet convent of Sadness. Forever
Cloistered, it spends its days and nights
With eyes closed, frail hands in a cross...

Lá fora, a Lua, Satanás, seduz!
Desdobra-se em requintes de Beleza...
É como um beijo ardente a Natureza...
A minha cela é como um rio de luz...

Fecha os teus olhos bem! Não vejas nada!
Empalidece mais! E, resignada,
Prende os teus braços a uma cruz maior!

Gela ainda a mortalha que te encerra!
Enche a boca de cinzas e de terra,
Ó minha mocidade toda em flor!

DA MINHA JANELA

Mar alto! Ondas quebradas e vencidas
Num soluçar aflito e murmurado...
Vôo de gaivotas, leve, imaculado,
Como neves nos píncaros nascidas!

Sol! Ave a tombar, asas já feridas,
Batendo ainda num arfar pausado...
Ó meu doce poente torturado
Rezo-te em mim, chorando, mãos erguidas!

Meu verso de Samain cheio de graça,
'Inda não és clarão já és luar
Como branco lilás que se desfaça!

Amor! Teu coração trago-o no peito...
Pulsa dentro de mim como este mar
Num beijo eterno, assim, nunca desfeito!...

The Moon outside, Satan, tempts me!
It blossoms into shimmers of Beauty…
Nature is like an ardent kiss…
My cell is like a river of light…

Shut tight your eyes! See nothing at all!
Turn yet paler! And, resigned,
Throw your arms around a greater cross!

Make the shroud that wraps you colder!
Fill your mouth with earth and ashes,
O my youth in your full flower!

FROM MY WINDOW

High sea! Vanquished waves
Breaking with whispered, troubled sighs…
Immaculate, weightless flight of gulls,
Like snows appearing on the hilltops!

Sun! A bird falling, still flapping
Its wounded wings while gasping for breath…
To you, sweet tortured sunset, I lift
My hands in inward prayer, weeping!

O my charming verse of Samain,
Not yet daylight, already you're moonlight,
Like a white lilac whose flowers wither!

Love! I carry your heart in my breast…
It pounds within me like this sea
In an endless, never withering kiss!...

EXALTAÇÃO

Viver!... Beber o vento e o sol!... Erguer
Ao céu os corações a palpitar!
Deus fez os nossos braços pra prender,
E a boca fez-se sangue pra beijar!

A chama, sempre rubra, ao alto, a arder!...
Asas sempre perdidas a pairar,
Mais alto para as estrelas desprender!...
A glória!... A fama!... O orgulho de criar!...

Da vida tenho o mel e tenho os travos
No lago dos meus olhos de violetas,
Nos meus beijos extáticos, pagãos!...

Trago na boca o coração dos cravos!
Boêmios, vagabundos, e poetas:
— Como eu sou vossa Irmã, ó meus Irmãos!...

SOU EU!

Pelos campos em fora, pelos combros,
Pelos montes que embalam a manhã,
Largo os meus rubros sonhos de pagã,
Enquanto as aves poisam nos meus ombros...

Em vão me sepultaram entre escombros
De catedrais duma escultura vã!
Olha-me o loiro sol tonto de assombros,
as nuvens, a chorar, chamam-me irmã!

EXALTATION

To live!... To drink the wind and sun!...
To lift up to the sky our throbbing
Hearts! God made our arms for grasping!
And gave us mouths of blood for kissing!

The always red-glowing flame on high!...
The always straying wings that soar
Still higher, ready to uproot the stars!...
Glory!... Fame!... The pride of creating!...

Life's honey and life's bitterness
Dwell in the lake of my eyes like violets
And in my ecstatic, pagan kisses!...

The heart of carnations fills my mouth!
O bohemians, tramps and poets,
How truly, Brothers, I am your Sister!

IT'S ME!

Over the fields, over the knolls,
Over the hills that cradle the morning,
I scatter my glowing pagan dreams
While birds alight on my shoulders...

In vain they buried me amid the rubble
Of vainly carved cathedrals! Dizzy
With wonder, the golden sun beholds me,
And the weeping clouds call me sister!

Ecos longínquos de ondas... de universos..
Ecos dum Mundo... dum distante Além,
Donde eu trouxe a magia dos meus versos!

Sou eu! Sou eu! A que nas mãos ansiosas
Prendeu da vida, assim como ninguém,
Os maus espinhos sem tocar nas rosas!

DEIXAI ENTRAR A MORTE

Deixai entrar a Morte, a Iluminada,
A que vem para mim, pra me levar.
Abri todas as portas par em par
Como asas a bater em revoada.

Que sou eu neste mundo?A deserdada,
A que prendeu nas mãos todo o luar,
A vida inteira, o sonho, a terra, o mar,
E que, ao abri-las, não encontrou nada!

Ó Mãe! Ó minha Mãe, pra que nasceste?
Entre agonias e em dores tamanhas
Pra que foi, dize lá, que me trouxeste

Dentro de ti?... Pra que eu tivesse sido
Somente o fruto amargo das entranhas
Dum lírio que em má hora foi nascido!...

Far echoes of waves… of universes…
Echoes of a World… of a distant Beyond,
From where I brought my verses' magic!

It's me! It's me! The one who, like no one,
Plucked from life with anxious hands
The hurtful thorns and none of the roses!

MAKE WAY FOR DEATH

Make way for Death, the Illuminated,
Who comes to take me from this world.
Fling wide open all the doors
Like flapping wings of birds in flight.

What am I here? The disinherited,
Who with her hands seized the moonlight,
The dream, the earth, the sea, all life,
Then opened her hands, and found nothing!

O Mother, dear Mother, why were you born?
Why, tell me, amidst such agonies
And horrid pains did you carry me

Inside you?... Just so that I could be
The bitter fruit that in evil hour
Was given birth by a lily's womb!...

OS PERIGOS DA INOCÊNCIA

Há poetas místicos de Deus as fêmeas
e há místicos tão machos que se julgam
o macho da fêmea quando são tangidos
pela vara do Espírito. E há quem sonhe
com anjos de viril adolescência,
e outros sonhando de anjos tão ambíguos
que não se sabe se no céu eles voam
de costas ou de frente. E há também quem julgue
que lá no Céu há-de dormir com a Mãe
como dormia em criança a separar o pai.
E também há os que não sonham nada,
e mal suspeitam que lhes acontece
(nos sexos de sua alma se esqueceram
de terem visto uma primeira vez
o pai e a mãe desnudos), quando Jeová

Jorge de Sena

1919–1978. Born in Lisbon. Entered Naval Academy at age 16 and made apprentice voyage that took him to ports in Africa. Earned a degree in Civil Engineering in Oporto (1944) and worked for 14 years as an engineer while pursuing literary activities, which included translating as well as writing. In 1959, fearing arrest and imprisonment for his involvement with the political opposition, he immigrated with his family (which would eventually include nine children) to Brazil, where he obtained his PhD in Literature and taught at several universities. Became an outspoken critic of the Salazar regime. Lived for the last thirteen years of his life in the United States, holding posts as a Professor of Portuguese at the University of Wisconsin and the University of California at Santa Barbara.

THE DANGERS OF INNOCENCE

There are mystical poets of God, female throughout,
and there are mystics so macho they think
that they're the macho in the female when touched
by the Spirit's wand. And there are those who
dream of virile adolescent angels,
while others dream of angels so ambiguous
one can't tell if they're flying through heaven
on their backs or bellies. And there are those who think
that there in heaven one will sleep with Mom
as one did in infancy, keeping Dad away.
And there are those who never dream at all,
and scarcely can imagine what they'll do
(in the sexes of their souls they quite forgot
first glimpsing Mom and Dad with nothing on)

as saias levantar diante deles
e lhes pregar o susto que Moisés levou.

ACÇÃO DE GRAÇAS

Às vezes, com minha filha no chão junto a mim,
fecho os olhos numa acção de graças...

Mas logo ela galreia,
nem isso me consente.

E regresso um pouco triste a uma alegria imensa.

AOS CINQUENTA ANOS...

Aos cinquenta anos sou um ser perplexo,
não como aos vinte, aos trinta, ou aos quarenta,
mas radicalmente perplexo. Não sei
se amo a vida ou a detesto. Se desejo
ou não desejo continuar vivendo.
Se amo ou não amo aqueles que amo,
se odeio ou não odeio os que detesto.
Se me quero patriarca, pai de família, como acabei sendo,
ou se me quero livre pelas ruas nocturnas
como quando não acabei de descobri-las
em décadas de andá-las, perseguindo
sequer o amor mas corpos, corpos, corpos.
Sou de Europa ou de América? De Portugal
ou Brasil? Desejo que toda a humanidade
seja feliz como queira, ou quero que ela morra
do cogumelo atómico prometido e possível?

when Jehovah lifts his skirts to them,
giving them the fright that Moses knew.

THANKSGIVING

Sometimes, with my daughter on the floor beside me,
I shut my eyes in giving thanks...

But soon enough she starts to babble,
Even this she won't allow me.

And I return, a bit sad, to an immense joy.

AT FIFTY...

At fifty I'm a confused being,
not like at twenty, thirty, or forty,
but profoundly confused. I don't know
if I love life or cannot stand it. If I want
or don't want to go on living.
If I love or don't love those whom I love,
if I hate or don't hate those I can't stand.
If I want to be a patriarch, a family man, as in fact I've ended up,
or if I want to be free in the night-time streets
as when I never finished exploring them
in decades of walking and walking, following,
if not love, then bodies, bodies, bodies.
Am I from Europe or America? From Portugal
or Brazil? Do I want all of mankind
to be happy as they wish to be, or do I hope they'll die
from the predicted, and distinctly possible, atomic mushroom?

Não sei. Definitivamente, não sei.
Julgas que estou deitado num leito de rosas?
— perguntava ao companheiro de tortura Cuauhtemoc.
Mas, mesmo destituído, preso e torturado,
ele era o Imperador, descendente dos deuses.
Eu não descendo dos deuses. O corpo dói-me,
que envelhece. O espírito dói-me de um cansaço físico.
As belezas de alma, seja de quem forem, deixaram de interessar-me.
Resta a poesia que me enoja nos outros
a não ser antigos, limpos agora do esterco
de terem vivido. E eu vivi tanto
que me parece tão pouco. E hei-de morrer
desesperado por não ter vivido. Aos 50 anos
nem sequer a raiva dos outros ainda me sustenta
o gosto e a paciência de estar vivo.
Outros que tentem e descubram:
que digam ou não digam é-me indiferente.

EM LOUVOR DA ITÁLIA

Roma, Veneza, Florença, Nápoles, *spaghetti*,
e os papas. Tanta beleza humana
numa terra dura e de ladrões.
Mas quantos séculos para estas pontes
e o jeito de roubar como de amar a vida
com tal volúpia que o roubado sente
o dever estrito de ficar mui grato.

I don't know. I simply don't know.
"You think I'm lying on a bed of roses?"
Cuauhtemoc asked the guy being tortured next to him.
But even dethroned, imprisoned, tortured,
he was the Emperor, a descendent of the gods.
I'm not descended from the gods. My body aches
from growing old. My spirit aches from physical exhaustion.
The beauties of the soul, whosesoever they may be, no longer interest me.
What's left is poetry, which sickens me in others,
but not the ancients, clean now of the dung
of having lived. And I've lived so much
it seems to me so little. And I shall die
desperate at not having lived. At fifty
not even the hatred of others still sustains in me
the patience to be, the pleasure of being alive.
Let others give it a try and see:
what they say or don't say is all the same to me.

IN PRAISE OF ITALY

Rome, Venice, Florence, Naples, spaghetti,
and the Popes. So much human beauty
in a land of hard soil and thieves.
But how many centuries for those bridges
and the knack of robbing just like loving life
with such voluptuousness that the robbed one feels
compelled to be filled with gratitude.

MARCHA FÚNEBRE DE SIEGFRIED
do *Crepúsculo dos Deuses*

Na tarde que de névoas se escurece
escuto a marcha que ao herói transporta
fúnebre e doce, tão violenta e fluida,
à sua pira em que arderá cadáver
a cinzas reduzido. Erguem-se os metais
nos ares entreabertos, terra se contrai
onde tambores reboam, e as madeiras
e cordas acompanham o cortejo
descendo para o rio que perpassa
igual sempre a si mesmo de outras águas
como os heróis que morrem tão humanos.
E é o que nos diz este mostrar por música:
os semi-deuses morrem como nós,
como nós sofrem mágoas de derrota,
e como nós desejam, amam, gozam
ou raivam da tristeza de não ter.
Mas nós não possuímos quanto a eles cabe,
neste fervor de imaginá-los, quem
nos cante o fim de tudo o que foi grande,
o que foi puro, o que de consentido
foi gesto dedicado sem usura
ao simples existir além de nós
na terra que nas trevas se nos fecha
de noite enevoada só distância
nas pálpebras cerradas deste corpo,
o herói que assassinado me transportam
neste cortejo em majestade e lágrimas.
Não temos isto mais do que em só música,
mas os deuses também não, que aos heróis mortos
nunca sobrevivem.

SIEGFRIED'S FUNERAL MARCH
from Wagner's ***Twilight of the Gods***

On an afternoon obscured by mists,
I listen to the march — sweetly sombre,
fluidly violent — that carries the hero
to the pyre where he'll burn, a corpse
reduced to ashes. The blaring brasses
half clear the air, the earth shrinks
where the drums boom, and the strings
and woodwinds accompany the procession
down to the river that flows forever
equal to itself with other waters,
like the heroes who die, so human.
And that's what this showing by music says:
the demigods die like us,
like us they are embittered by defeat,
and like us they yearn, love and revel
or they seethe with sorrow at having failed.
But we don't have all they have, in our zeal
to imagine them. We don't have anyone
to sing for us the end of whatever was great,
whatever was pure, whatever was as far
as permitted a disinterested act dedicated
to simply existing beyond ourselves
in this land that wraps us in darkness
on a misty night, nothing but distance
in the lowered eyelids of this corpse,
the assassinated hero they carry for me
in this majestic and tearful procession.
We do not have this except in mere music,
but neither do the gods, whom dead heroes
succeed in outliving.

O DESEJADO TÚMULO

Numa azinhaga escura de arrabalde
haveis de sepultar-me. Que o meu túmulo
seja o lugar escuso para encontros.
Que o jovem desesperado e solitário
vagueando venha masturbar-se ali;
que o namorado sem um quarto aonde
leve ao castigo a namorada, a traga
e a force e a viole sobre a minha tumba;
que o invertido venha ajoelhar-se
à beira dela ante quem esperma vende,
ou deite abaixo as calças e se entregue,
as mãos buscando apoio nessa pedra.
Que bandos de malandros ali tragam
a rapariga que raptaram, e
a deixem lá estendida a escorrer sangue.
Que as prostitutas reles, piolhosas,
na laje pinguem corrimentos quando
a pobres velhos se venderam lá.
E que as crianças que brincando venham
jogar à minha volta, sem pisar nos cantos
a trampa mais cheirosa do que a morte
e que é memória humana de azinhagas,
ali descubram, mal adivinhando,
as nódoas secas do que foi violência,
ou foi desejo ou o que se chama vício
e as lavem rindo com seu mijo quente
a rechinar na pedra que me cobre
(e regressem um dia a repeti-las).

THE DESIRED TOMB

You shall bury me in some obscure
back alley on the edge of town. May my tomb
be the secluded place where lovers meet.
May the desperate, lonely youth
adrift, come there to masturbate;
may the boy without a room in which
to give his girlfriend what she deserves
bring her there, force, rape her there upon my tomb;
may the queer come and kneel
beside my grave before the one who sells him sperm,
or let his pants down and surrender,
his hands in search of buttress on this stone.
May bands of punks drag
the girl they've abducted
and leave her stretched out here, bathed in blood.
May lousy, sleazy prostitutes
drip discharge on my slab,
while they sell themselves to poor old men.
And may children who come to play
their games around me, never stepping on
the turds in corners, more fragrant than death,
mankind's memorial to hidden lanes,
there discover, barely understood,
dried stains of what was violence,
or what desire, or what's called vice
and, laughing, wash them off, with their warm piss
splattering on the stone that covers me
(and may they come again one day to do it all again).

PRAIA

Os pinheiros gemem quando passa o vento
O sol bate no chão e as pedras ardem.

Longe caminham os deuses fantásticos do mar
Brancos de sal e brilhantes como peixes.

Pássaros selvagens de repente,
Atirados contra a luz como pedradas,
Sobem e morrem no céu verticalmente
E o seu corpo é tomado nos espaços.

As ondas marram quebrando contra a luz
A sua fronte ornada de colunas.

E uma antiquíssima nostalgia de ser mastro
Baloiça nos pinheiros.

Sophia de Mello Breyner

1919–2004. Born in Oporto. Studied Classical Philology at the University of Lisbon (1936–39), without taking a degree. In the late 1940s she settled for good in Lisbon, where she raised five children. In the 1960s she became one of the leading voices among progressive Catholics who opposed the dictatorial regime in Portugal and the colonial wars in Africa. Translator of plays and poetry into Portuguese.

BEACH

The pine trees creak when the wind passes
The sun strikes the ground and the stones burn.

White with salt and gleaming like fish
The fantastic sea gods pass in the distance.

Swift wild birds, thrown
Against the light like a spray of pebbles,
Rise and die straight up into the sky,
Their bodies swallowed by space.

The rushing waves break against the light
Their foreheads adorned with columns.

And an ancient nostalgia for being masts
Sways in the pines.

LUSITÂNIA

Os que avançam de frente para o mar
E nele enterram como uma aguda faca
A proa negra dos seus barcos
Vivem de pouco pão e de luar

ESCUTO

Escuto mas não sei
Se o que oiço é silêncio
Ou deus

Escuto sem saber se estou ouvindo
O ressoar das planícies do vazio
Ou a consciência atenta
Que nos confins do universo
Me decifra e fita

Apenas sei que caminho como quem
É olhado amado e conhecido
E por isso em cada gesto ponho
Solenidade e risco

O HOSPITAL E A PRAIA

E eu caminhei no hospital
Onde o branco é desolado e sujo
Onde o branco é a cor que fica onde não há cor
E onde a luz é cinza

LUSITANIA

Those who advance against the sea
Driving into it like a whetted blade
The black prow of their wooden boats
Live off moonlight and a little bread

I LISTEN

I listen without knowing
If what I hear is silence
Or god

I listen but don't know if I'm hearing
The echo of the empty expanses
Or the attentive consciousness
Which from the edge of the universe
Sees and deciphers me

I know only that I walk as one
Who is watched loved and known
And that's why I place in the smallest act
Solemnity and risk

THE HOSPITAL AND THE BEACH

And I walked through the hospital
With its desolate dirty whiteness
The colour that remains where there is no colour
And where the light is ash

E eu caminhei nas praias e nos campos
O azul do mar e o roxo da distância
Enrolei-os em redor do meu pescoço
Caminhei na praia quase livre como um deus

Não perguntei por ti à pedra meu Senhor
Nem me lembrei de ti bebendo o vento
O vento era vento e a pedra pedra
E isso inteiramente me bastava

E nos espaços da manhã marinha
Quase livre como um deus eu caminhava

E todo o dia vivi como uma cega

Porém no hospital eu vi o rosto
Que não é pinheiral nem é rochedo
E vi a luz como cinza na parede
E vi a dor absurda e desmedida

ANTÍNOO

Sob o peso nocturno dos cabelos
Ou sob a lua diurna do teu ombro
Procurei a ordem intacta do mundo
A palavra não ouvida

Longamente sob o fogo ou sob o vidro
Procurei no teu rosto
A revelação dos deuses que não sei

Porém passaste através de mim
Como passamos através da sombra

And I walked over beaches and fields
Wrapping around my neck
The ocean's blue and the horizon's purple
I walked on the beach almost free as a god

I didn't ask for you at the stone my Lord
I didn't remember you as I drank the wind
The wind was wind and the stone stone
And that satisfied me completely

And in the ocean morning's open spaces
Almost free as a god I walked

And I lived every day as if I were blind

But in the hospital I saw the face
That's not a high rock nor a forest of pines
And I saw the light like ash on the wall
And I saw absurd immeasurable pain

ANTINOUS

Under the nocturnal weight of your hair
Under the diurnal moon of your shoulder
I sought the unbroken order of the world
The word not heard

Time and again under fire or glass
I sought in your face
The revelation of gods I don't know

But you passed through me
As we pass through shade

TORSO

Torcendo o torso virava o volante da escavadora
Ao cair da tarde num Setembro do século XX
Na estrada que vai de Patras para Atenas

Combatia no poente sua beleza helenística
As massas musculares inchadas pelo esforço
Construíam o tumulto de clarão e sombra
Que dobra os corpos dos deuses já perdidos
Dos frisos de Pérgamo

Pois também no poente onde eu habito
Os deuses são vencidos

O MINOTAURO

Em Creta
Onde o Minotauro reina
Banhei-me no mar

Há uma rápida dança que se dança em frente de um toiro
Na antiquíssima juventude do dia

Nenhuma droga me embriagou me escondeu me protegeu
Só bebi retsina tendo derramado na terra a parte que pertence
aos deuses

De Creta
Enfeitei-me de flores e mastiguei o amargo vivo das ervas
Para inteiramente acordada comungar a terra
De Creta
Beijei o chão como Ulisses
Caminhei na luz nua

TORSO

His twisting torso turned the bulldozer wheels
At twilight in a twentieth-century September
On the road from Patras to Athens

In the sunset his Hellenistic beauty struggled
The bulging muscles of his straining arms
Composed the tumult of light and shadow
That bends the bodies of the doomed gods
In the Pergamum friezes

Likewise in the sunset that I inhabit
The gods have been defeated

THE MINOTAUR

In Crete
Where the Minotaur reigns
I swam in the sea

There's a dance that is nimbly danced before a bull
In the anciently youthful day

No drug entranced me hid me protected me
I drank only retsina and poured on the ground the gods' portion

In Crete
I wore flowers and chewed the fresh bitterness of herbs
To be fully awake as I partook of the earth
In Crete
I kissed the ground like Ulysses
I walked in the naked light

Devastada era eu própria como a cidade em ruína
Que ninguém reconstruiu
Mas no sol dos meus pátios vazios
A fúria reina intacta
E penetra comigo no interior do mar
Porque pertenço à raça daqueles que mergulham de olhos abertos
E reconhecem o abismo pedra a pedra anêmona a anêmona flor
a flor
E o mar de Creta por dentro é todo azul
Oferenda incrível de primordial alegria
Onde o sombrio Minotauro navega

Pinturas ondas colunas e planícies
Em Creta
Inteiramente acordada atravessei o dia
E caminhei no interior dos palácios veementes e vermelhos
Palácios sucessivos e roucos
Onde se ergue o respirar de sussurrada treva
E nos fitam pupilas semi-azuis de penumbra e terror
Imanentes ao dia —
Caminhei no palácio dual de combate e confronto
Onde o Príncipe dos Lírios ergue os seus gestos matinais

Nenhuma droga me embriagou me escondeu me protegeu
O Dionysos que dança comigo na vaga não se vende em
nenhum mercado negro
Mas cresce uma flor daqueles cujo ser
Sem cessar se busca e se perde se desune e se reúne
E esta é a dança do ser

Em Creta
Os muros de tijolo da cidade minoica
São feitos de barro amassado com algas
E quando me virei para trás da minha sombra
Vi que era azul o sol que tocava o meu ombro

I too was devastated like the ruined city
No one ever rebuilt
But in the sunlight of my empty courts
Fury reigns intact
And with me it penetrates into the sea's core
For I belong to the race of those who dive in with eyes open
To survey the depths one stone one anemone one flower at a
time
And the sea of Crete is all blue inside
An incredible offering of primordial joy
Where the Minotaur darkly moves

Paintings waves columns and plains
In Crete
Fully awake I went through the day
And walked in fierce vermillion palaces
Hoarse successive palaces
Where the breathing of whispered darkness heaves
And we're watched by bluish eyes of shadow and terror
Immanent in the day —
I walked in the dual palace of struggle and confrontation
Where the Prince of Lilies lifts his hands as weightless as morning

No drug entranced me hid me protected me
The Dionysus who dances with me in the wave isn't for sale in
any black market
But grows like the flower of those whose being
Seeks and gets lost is shattered and reunited
And this is the dance of being

In Crete
The brick walls of Minoan cities
Are made of clay and seaweed
And when I turned around to my shadow
I saw that the sun on my shoulder was blue

Em Creta onde o Minotauro reina atravessei a vaga
De olhos abertos inteiramente acordada
Sem drogas e sem filtro
Só vinho bebido em frente da solenidade das coisas —
Porque pertenço à raça daqueles que percorrem o labirinto
Sem jamais perderem o fio de linho da palavra

RESSURGIREMOS

Ressurgiremos ainda sob os muros de Cnossos
E em Delphos centro do mundo
Ressurgiremos ainda na dura luz de Creta

Ressurgiremos ali onde as palavras
São o nome das coisas
E onde são claros e vivos os contornos
Na aguda luz de Creta

Ressurgiremos ali onde pedra estrela e tempo
São o reino do homem
Ressurgiremos para olhar para a terra de frente
Na luz limpa de Creta

Pois convém tornar claro o coração do homem
E erguer a negra exactidão da cruz
Na luz branca de Creta

In Crete where the Minotaur reigns I went through the wave
Eyes open fully awake
Without drugs or a potion
Just the wine I drank and the solemnity of things
For I belong to the race of those who wend through the labyrinth
Without ever losing the linen thread of the word

WE WILL RISE

We will rise again beneath the walls of Knossos
And in Delphi the centre of the world
We will rise again in the harsh light of Crete

We will rise where words
Are the names of things
Where outlines are clear and vivid
There in the sharp light of Crete

We will rise where stone the stars and time
Are the kingdom of man
We will rise to stare straight at the earth
In the clean light of Crete

For it is good to clarify the heart of man
And to lift the black exactness of the cross
In the white light of Crete

from ESTALACTITE

I

O céu calcário
duma colina oca,
donde morosas gotas
de água ou de pedra
hão-de cair
daqui a alguns milênios
e acordar
as ténues flores
nas corolas de cal
tão próximas de mim
que julgo ouvir,
filtrado pelo túnel
do tempo, da colina,
o orvalho num jardim.

Carlos de Oliveira

1921–1981. Born in Belém do Pará, Brazil, to two Portuguese immigrants. Returned with family to Portugal at the age of two. Studied History and Philosophy at the University of Coimbra, graduating in 1947 with a thesis titled *Contribution to a Neo-Realist Aesthetics*. Spent rest of adult life in Lisbon. Dividing his creative energy between fiction, poetry and visual art, he was a paramount figure of Portuguese Neo-Realism, a movement founded in the early 1940s to promote literature that foregrounded economic disparities and social injustices.

---

from STALACTITE

I

The limestone sky
of the hollow hill,
where sullen drops
of water or of stone
will fall
a few millennia from now
and waken
tenuous flowers
in calcified corollas
so close to me
I think I hear,
filtering through the tunnel
of time, and of this hill,
the garden's dew.

II
Imaginar
o som do orvalho,
a lenta contracção
das pétalas,
o peso da água
a tal distância,
registar
nessa memória
ao contrário
o ritmo da pedra
dissolvida
quando poisa
gota a gota
nas flores antecipadas.

III
Se o poema
analisasse
a própria oscilação
interior,
cristalizasse
um outro movimento
mais subtil,
o da estrutura
em que se geram
milênios depois
estas imaginárias
flores calcárias,
acharia
o seu micro-rigor.

IV
Localizar
na frágil espessura

II
To imagine
the sound of dew,
the slow contraction
of petals,
the weight of water
at such a distance,
to register
in that inverted
memory
the rhythm of dissolving
stone
as it settles
drop by drop
on those anticipated flowers.

III
If the poem
were to analyse
its own internal
oscillation,
to crystallize
another, more subtle
motion,
that of a structure
in which
millennia later
those imaginary
calcified flowers
are engendered,
it would find
its micro-clarity.

IV
To find
in the fragile thickness

do tempo,
que a linguagem
pôs
em vibração,
o ponto morto
onde a velocidade
se fractura
e aí
determinar
com exactidão
o foco
do silêncio.

V
Espaço
para caírem
gotas de água
ou pedra
levadas
pelo seu peso,
suaves acidentes
da colina
silenciosa para
a cal
florir
nesta caligrafia
de pétalas
e letras.

VI
Algures
o poema sonha
o arquétipo
do voo
inutilmente

of time,
that language sets
to pulsing,
the eye of stillness
where velocity
breaks apart
and from there
determine
with exactitude
the focal point
of silence.

V

Space
so that
drops of water
or of stone may fall
carried
by their weight,
smooth angularities
of the silent
hill
so limestone
may flower
in this calligraphy
of petals
and of letters.

VI

Somewhere
the poem dreams
the archetype
of flight
in vain

porque repete
apenas
o signo, o desenho
do outono
aéreo
onde se perde a asa
quando vier
o instante
de voar.

VII
O pulsar
das palavras,
atraídas
ao chão
desta colina
por uma densidade
que palpita
entre
a cal
e a água,
lembra
o das estrelas
antes
de caírem.

for it merely
repeats
the sign, the pattern
of airy
autumn
in which the bird is lost
just
at the moment
of flight.

VII

The pulsing
of words,
attracted
to the surface
of this hill
by a density
that throbs
between
limestone
and water,
reminiscent of
the pulsing of stars
before
they fall.

CORPO HABITADO

Corpo num horizonte de água,
corpo aberto
à lenta embriaguez dos dedos,
corpo defendido
pelo fulgor das maçãs,
rendido de colina em colina,
corpo amorosamente humedecido
pelo sol dócil da língua.

Corpo com gosto a erva rasa
de secreto jardim,
corpo onde entro em casa,
corpo onde me deito
para sugar o silêncio,
ouvir
o rumor das espigas,

Eugénio de Andrade

1923–2005. Pseudonym of José Fontinhas. Born near Fundão, in central Portugal. Moved to Lisbon when he was ten years old and to Coimbra when he was twenty. From 1950 until his death he lived in Oporto. Worked for many years as a civil servant. Published translations from García Lorca (1946), whose poetry influenced his own.

INHABITED BODY

Body on a horizon of water,
body open
to the slow intoxication of fingers,
body defended
by the splendour of apples,
surrendered hill by hill,
body lovingly made moist
by the tongue's pliant sun.

Body with the taste of cropped grass
in a secret garden,
body where I am at home,
body where I lie down
to suck up silence,
to hear
the murmur of blades of grain,

respirar
a doçura escuríssima das silvas.

Corpo de mil bocas,
e todas fulvas de alegria,
todas para sorver,
todas para morder até que um grito
irrompa das entranhas,
e suba às torres,
e suplique um punhal.
Corpo para entregar às lágrimas.
Corpo para morrer.

Corpo para beber até ao fim —
meu oceano breve
e branco,
minha secreta embarcação,
meu vento favorável,
minha vária, sempre incerta
navegação.

VIAGEM

Iremos juntos separados.
as palavras mordidas uma a uma,
taciturnas, cintilantes
— ó meu amor, constelação de bruma,
ombro dos meus braços hesitantes.
Esquecidos, lembrados, repetidos
na boca dos amantes que se beijam
no alto dos navios;
desfeitos ambos, ambos inteiros,
no rasto dos peixes luminosos,
afogados na voz dos marinheiros.

to breathe
the deep dark sweetness of the bramble bush.

Body of a thousand mouths,
all tawny with joy,
all ready to sip,
ready to bite till a scream
bursts from the bowels
and mounts to the towers
and pleads for a dagger.
Body for surrendering to tears.
Body ripe for death.

Body for imbibing to the end —
my ocean, brief
and white,
my secret vessel,
my propitious wind,
my errant, unknown,
endless navigation.

VOYAGE

Side by side and separate we'll go,
and bite our words, as one by one they come,
taciturn and brilliantly aglow
— oh love, my constellation of pure mist,
shoulder of my hesitating arms.
Forgotten, remembered, then named again
in mouths of lovers now who kiss
high upon the decks of passing ships;
both of us undone, scattered deep on shale,
floating whole in realms of radiant fish,
and drowned in seamen's voices as they sail.

É UM LUGAR AO SUL, um lugar onde
a cal
amotinada desafia o olhar.
Onde viveste. Onde às vezes no sono

vives ainda. O nome prenhe de água
escorre-te da boca.
Por caminhos de cabras descias
à praia, o mar batia

naquelas pedras, nestas sílabas.
Os olhos perdiam-se afigados
no clarão
do último ou do primeiro dia.

Era a perfeição.

AS CASAS entram pela água,
a porta do pátio aberta à estrela
matutina, em flor
os espinheiros,

nas janelas apenas a cintilação
juvenil do mar antigo,
esse que viu ainda as naves
do mais errante de quantos marinheiros

perderam norte e razão
a contemplar a reflectida estrela
da manhã:
só na morte não somos estrangeiros.

IT'S A PLACE IN THE SOUTH, a place where whiteness
gone wild stares you in the eye.
Where you lived. Where sometimes in sleep

you are living still. The name heavy with water
drips from your mouth.
Along goat paths you dropped
to the beach, the sea pounding

those stones, these syllables.
Eyes lost themselves, drowned
in the dazzle
of the last or the very first day.

Perfection.

THE HOUSES enter the water,
front gates open to the morning
star, hawthorns
in blossom,

in the windows just the youthful
shimmer of an ancient sea,
the one that watched the ships
of the farthest straying seamen

blinded to compass and reason
contemplating the reflected
morning star:
only in death are we no longer strangers.

IGNORO O QUE seja a flor da água
Mas conheço o seu aroma:
depois das primeiras chuvas
sobe ao terraço,

entra nu pela varanda,
o corpo inda molhado
procura o nosso corpo e começa a tremer:
então é como se na sua boca

um resto de imortalidade
nos fosse dado a beber,
e toda a música da terra,
toda a música do céu fosse nossa,

até ao fim do mundo,
até amanhecer.

SOBRE A MESA a fruta arde: peras,
laranjas, maçãs, pressentem
a íntima brancura
dos dentes, o desejo represado,

o espesso vinho de vozes antigas;
arde a melancolia ao inventar
outra cidade,
outro país, outros céus onde lançar

os olhos e o riso: deita-te comigo,
trago-te do mar
a crespa luz da espuma,
nos flancos este amor retido.

I DON'T KNOW what a water-flower is,
but I know its scent:
after the first rains
it rises to the terrace,

enters, naked, the house,
its body still wet,
and, searching out our body, begins to tremble:
then it is as if in its mouth

a residue of immortality
were given us to drink,
and all the music of earth,
all the music of the heavens were ours,

to the end of the world,
till the coming of dawn.

UPON THE TABLE the fruit burns: pears,
oranges, apples already sense
the intimate whiteness
of teeth, the restrained desire,

the thick wine of ancient voices;
melancholy burns as it invents
another city,
another country, other skies for us to cast

our eyes toward and a laugh: lie down with me,
I bring you from the sea
the crinkled light of the foam;
in my loins this straightened flame.

SÓ O CAVALO, só aqueles olhos grandes
de criança, aquela
profusão da seda, me fazem falta.
Não é a voz,

que tanto escutei, escura do rio,
nem a cintura fresca,
a primeira onde pousei a mão,
e conheci o amor;

é esse olhar que de noite em noite vem
da lonjura por algum atalho,
e me rouba o sono,
e não me poupa o coração.

Meu coração, alentejo de orvalho.

CONTRAPONTO

Oiço-a ainda longe, a neve.
Vai chegar um dia com a luz de novembro,
antes passará pelos teus lábios.
E serás condescendente,
a ponto de lhe indicares o caminho
mais longo,
o que leva ao bosque onde
te peguei na mão
sem coragem para a levar à boca.
A neve tem esse lado acolhedor
de farol no escuro.
Antes de nos soterrar o coração.

JUST THE HORSE, just those wide
child's eyes, that
profusion of silk, that's all I miss.
Not the dark river

voice I always listened to,
nor the cool waist,
the first I laid my hand upon,
knowing love;

it's that gaze that comes, night after night,
along some bypath from afar,
and steals my sleep,
and will not spare my heart.

My heart, a prairie covered in dew.

COUNTERPOINT

I hear it still far off, the snow.
It will come one day with the light of November,
but first it will have passed through your lips.
And you will be kind enough
to indicate to it
the longest way,
that which leads to the woods where
I took your hand
without the courage to lift it to my mouth.
Snow has that comforting feel
of a lighthouse in the dark.
Before it buries our heart.

OS FRUTOS

Assim eu queria o poema:
fremente de luz, áspero de terra,
rumoroso de águas e de vento.

OUTROS RITMOS, OUTROS MODOS

Não é o mar, não é o vento, é o sol
que me dói da cintura aos sapatos.
Sol de fins de julho,
ou de agosto a prumo: finas
agulhas de aço.

É o sol destes dias, aceso
na folhagem.
Bebendo a minha água.
Colado à minha pele.

É doutro território, doutro areal.
Tem outros ritmos, outros modos,
outros vagares para roer
a cal, morder-me os olhos.
Até quando cega canta ao arder.

THE FRUIT

This is how I want the poem to be:
trembling with light, coarse with earth,
murmuring with waters and with wind.

OTHER RHYTHMS, OTHER MODES

It isn't the sea, it isn't the wind, it's the sun
that aches in me from my waist to my shoes.
The sun of late July,
or perpendicular in August: fine
needles of steel.

It is the sun of these days, burning
in the foliage.
Drinking my water.
Stuck to my skin.

It's from another realm, another stretch of sand.
It has other rhythms, other modes,
other lazing times in which to gnaw
limestone, bite my eyes.
Even as it blinds, it sings as it burns.

POEMA

Faz-se luz pelo processo
de eliminação de sombras
Ora as sombras existem
as sombras têm exaustiva vida própria
não dum e doutro lado da luz mas do próprio seio dela
intensamente amantes   loucamente amadas
e espalham pelo chão braços de luz cinzenta
que se introduzem pelo bico nos olhos do homem

Por outro lado a sombra dita a luz
não ilumina   realmente   os objectos
os objectos vivem às escuras
numa perpétua aurora surrealista
com a qual não podemos contactar
senão como os amantes

Mário Cesariny

1923–2006. Born in Lisbon. Studied Fine Arts as an adolescent and became a notable painter as well as a poet. He initially associated with the Portuguese Neo-Realists but was soon disenchanted, finding them ideologically too dogmatic. Attracted to surrealism, he met André Breton while studying at an art school in Paris. In 1947 he and others, including Alexandre O'Neill, founded the Portuguese Surrealist movement. This split into two rival groups, both of which dissipated in the early 1950s, but the spirit of the movement lived on in the work of individual poets, especially Cesariny, who published theoretical texts on surrealism and compiled anthologies of Portuguese Surrealist writings. In his last years he quit writing and dedicated himself exclusively to visual art.

POEM

Light occurs through the process
of eliminating shadows
Shadows are what exist
they have their own exhaustive life
not on this or that side of the light but at its very core
intensely loving   insanely loved
and they spread over the ground their arms of grey light
that enter human eyes at the corners

Nor does the shadow called light
illuminate   in reality   objects
objects live in the dark
in a perpetual surrealist aurora
we can have no contact with
except in the way of lovers

de olhos fechados
e lâmpadas nos dedos   e na boca

YOU ARE WELCOME TO ELSINORE

Entre nós e as palavras há metal fundente
entre nós e as palavras há hélices que andam
e podem dar-nos morte   violar-nos   tirar
do mais fundo de nós o mais útil segredo
entre nós e as palavras há perfis ardentes
espaços cheios de gente de costas
altas flores venenosas   portas por abrir
e escadas e ponteiros e crianças sentadas
à espera do seu tempo e do seu precipício

Ao longo da muralha que habitamos
há palavras de vida   há palavras de morte
há palavras imensas, que esperam por nós
e outras, frágeis, que deixaram de esperar
há palavras acesas como barcos
e há palavras homens, palavras que guardam
o seu segredo e a sua posição
Entre nós e as palavras, surdamente,
as mãos e as paredes de Elsinore

E há palavras nocturnas palavras gemidos
palavras que nos sobem ilegíveis à boca
palavras diamantes palavras nunca escritas
palavras impossíveis de escrever
por não termos connosco cordas de violinos
nem todo o sangue do mundo nem todo o amplexo do ar
e os braços dos amantes escrevem muito alto
muito além do azul onde oxidados morrem
palavras maternais só sombra só soluço

with eyes closed
and lamps in our fingers   lamps on our lips

YOU ARE WELCOME TO ELSINORE

Between us and words there is molten metal
between us and words there are spinning propellers
and they can kill us   ravish us   extract
from deep down in us the most valuable secret
between us and words there are burning looks
spaces full of people with their backs turned
tall poisonous flowers   closed doors
stairways clocks ticking and children sitting
waiting for their time and their precipice

Along the walls in which we live
there are words of life   there are words of death
there are enormous words that wait for us
and other, fragile words that have stopped waiting
there are words lit up like boats
and there are words that are men, words that conceal
what they mean and where they stand
Between us and words, without a sound,
the hands and walls of Elsinore

And there are words of the night words that are moans
illegible words that rise to our lips
diamond words never yet written
words that cannot be written
because we would need to have strings of violins
all the world's blood and the air's endless embracing
and in the highest reaches, beyond the blue where
they rust and die, the arms of lovers write
maternal words just shadow just sobbing

só espasmos só amor só solidão desfeita

Entre nós e as palavras, os emparedados
e entre nós e as palavras, o nosso querer falar

O NAVIO DE ESPELHOS
não navega, cavalga

Seu mar é a floresta
que lhe serve de nível

Ao crepúsculo espelha
sol e lua nos flancos

Por isso o tempo gosta
de deitar-se com ele

Os armadores não amam
a sua rota clara

Vista do movimento
dir-se-ia que pára

Quando chega à cidade
nenhum cais o abriga

O seu porão traz nada
nada leva à partida

Vozes e ar pesado
é tudo o que transporta

E no mastro espelhado
uma espécie de porta

just spasms just love just devastated solitude

Between us and words: people walled in
and between us and words: our wanting to speak

THE SHIP OF MIRRORS

doesn't sail, it gallops

Its sea is the forest
forming a level plane

At twilight its broadsides
mirror sun and moon

That's why time loves
to lie down with it

Ship owners don't like
the clear course it cruises

To someone in motion
it seems to stand still

When it reaches the city
no wharf takes it in

Arriving or departing
its hold contains nothing

Voices and heavy air
are all it transports

And a species of door
in its mirrored mast

Seus dez mil capitães
têm o mesmo rosto

A mesma cinta escura
o mesmo grau e posto

Quando um se revolta
há dez mil insurrectos

(Como os olhos da mosca
reflectem os objectos)

E quando um deles ala
o corpo sobe os mastros
e escruta o mar do fundo

Toda a nave cavalga
(como no espaço os astros)

Do princípio do mundo
até ao fim do mundo

POEMA

Tu estás em mim como eu estive no berço
com a árvore sob a sua crosta
como o navio no fundo do mar

Its ten thousand captains
all have the same face

The same dark belt
the same rank and office

One rebel sailor equals
ten thousand mutineers

(In the same way the eyes
of a fly reflect objects)

And when one of them hoists
his body up the masts
and scans the ocean depths

The whole ship gallops
(like the stars in space)

From the world's beginning
to the world's end

POEM

You are in me as I was in a crib
as the tree is within the bark
as the ship is at the bottom of the sea

BEING BEAUTEOUS

O meu amigo inglês que entrou no quarto da cama e correu
de um só gesto todas as cortinas
sabia o que corria
digo disse direis era vergonha
era sermos estranhos   mais do que isso: estrangeiros
e tão perto um do outro naquela casa
mas eu vejo maior   mais escuro dentro do corpo
e descobri que a luz é coisa de ricos
gente que passa a vida a olhar para o sol
cultivar abelhas no sexo   liras na cabeça
e mal a noite tinge a faixa branca da praia
vai a correr telefonar para a polícia

E não bem pelas jóias de diamante os serviços de bolso e as
criadas
digo ricos de espírito
ricos de experiência
ricos de saber bem como decorre
para um lado o sémen para o outro a caca
e nos doces intervalares
a urina as bibliotecas as estações o teatro
tudo o que já amado
e arrecadado no canto do olho a implorar mais luz para ter sido
verdade

O meu amigo inglês não se lembrava
senão dos gestos simples do começo
e corria as cortinas e criava
para além do beijo flébil que podemos
a viagem sem fim e sem regresso

BEING BEAUTEOUS

My English friend who entered the bedroom and drew
the curtains with a single swipe
knew what he was drawing
I say he said you'll say it was shocking
it was the fact we were strangers   strangers and foreigners
and so close to each other in that house
but I see more deeply   more darkly inside the body
and I've discovered that light is for the rich
those who spend their lives gazing at the sun
keeping bees in their sex organs   lyres in their heads
and no sooner does night touch the white strip of beach
than they run and phone the police

Forget diamond jewellery amenities and housemaids
I'm talking about rich in spirit
rich in experience
rich in knowing how
semen flows out one side and faeces out the other
and in the sweet in-betweens
there's urine and libraries train stations the theatre
all that has been loved
and stored in the corner of an eye imploring more light for it to
have been true

My English friend remembered only
the simple gestures for starting out
and he drew the curtains and created
beyond the feeble kiss we can kiss
the endless voyage of no return

PERFILADOS DE MEDO

Perfilados de medo, agradecemos
o medo que nos salva da loucura.
Decisão e coragem valem menos
e a vida sem viver é mais segura.

Aventureiros já sem aventura,
perfilados de medo combatemos
irónicos fantasmas à procura
do que não fomos, do que não seremos.

Perfilados de medo, sem mais voz,
o coração nos dentes oprimido,
os loucos, os fantasmas somos nós.

Rebanho pelo medo perseguido,
já vivemos tão juntos e tão sós
que da vida perdemos o sentido...

Alexandre O'Neill

1924–1986. Born in Lisbon, his surname came from an Irish ancestor. Quit nautical school after the first year, since his short-sightedness prevented him from obtaining a pilot's license. One of the founders of the Portuguese surrealist movement (1947), he distanced himself from it in his first book of poems (1951) but acknowledged that some of its artistic principles influenced his work. Earned his living through writing, as a newspaper critic, scriptwriter, and publicist. A resolute individualist, he refused to join any of the political opposition movements, though he was highly critical of the Salazar regime, which closely monitored his activities.

STANDING AT FEARFUL ATTENTION

Standing at fearful attention, we're grateful
to fear, which keeps us from going mad.
Decision and courage are bad
for our health; life without living is safer.

Explorers whose exploits are history,
standing in fear we struggle against
ironic ghosts in our ongoing quest
for what we weren't and never will be.

Standing in fear with no voice of our own,
just teeth that gnash on our hearts in fury,
we are the madmen, we are the ghosts.

A flock of sheep pursued by fear,
we live so together and so alone
that life's meaning has disappeared.

A HISTÓRIA DA MORAL

Você tem-me cavalgado,
seu safado!
Você tem-me cavalgado,
mas nem por isso me pôs
a pensar como você.

Que uma coisa pensa o cavalo;
outra quem está a montá-lo.

PORTUGAL

Ó Portugal, se fosses só três sílabas,
linda vista para o mar,
Minho verde, Algarve de cal,
jerico rapando o espinhaço da terra,
surdo e miudinho,
moinho a braços com um vento
testarudo, mas embolado e, afinal, amigo,
se fosses só o sal, o sol, o sul,
o ladino pardal,
o manso boi coloquial,
a rechinante sardinha,
a desancada varina,
o plumitivo ladrilhado de lindos adjectivos,
a muda queixa amendoada
duns olhos pestanítidos,
se fosses só a cegarrega do estio, dos estilos,
o ferrugento cão asmático das praias,
o grilo engaiolado, a grila no lábio,
o calendário na parede, o emblema na lapela,

THE HISTORY OF MORALITY

You've mounted me and there you sit,
you rotten shit!
You've mounted me and there you sit,
but even that won't really make
me think like you.

For the horse thinks one way as he strides;
thoughts quite different from the one who rides.

PORTUGAL

If only, Portugal, you were just three syllables,
a beautiful view of the sea,
the green Minho, the whitewashed Algarve,
a tiny, tranquil donkey
foraging on the mountain ridge,
a mill swinging its arms at a wind as stubborn
as a bull but with padded horns and after all friendly,
if only you were just salt, sun, the south,
the shrewd sparrow,
the meek colloquial ox,
the sizzling sardine,
the waddling fishwife,
the scribbler bundled up in pretty adjectives,
the silent, almondish complaint
of sharp eyes with black lashes,
if only you were just the buzzing of summer, the buzz of fashion,
the decrepit asthmatic dog of beaches,
the caged cricket, the cagey customer,
the calendar on the wall, the pin on a lapel,

ó Portugal, se fosses só três sílabas
de plástico, que era mais barato!

*

Doceiras de Amarante, barristas de Barcelos,
rendeiras de Viana, toureiros da Golegã,
não há "papo-de-anjo" que seja o meu derriço,
galo que cante a cores na minha prateleira,
alvura arrendada para o meu devaneio,
bandarilha que possa enfeitar-me o cachaço.

Portugal: questão que eu tenho comigo mesmo,
golpe até ao osso, fome sem entretém,
perdigueiro marrado e sem narizes, sem perdizes,
rocim engraxado,
feira cabisbaixa,
meu remorso,
meu remorso de todos nós...

DE PORTA EM PORTA

— Quem? O infinito?
Diz-lhe que entre.
Faz bem ao infinito
estar entre gente.

— Uma esmola? Coxeia?
Ao que ele chegou!
Podes dar-lhe a bengala
que era do avô.

if only, Portugal, you were just three syllables
made of plastic, which would be cheaper!

*

Confectioners of Amarante, potters from Barcelos,
lace-makers of Viana, bullfighters from Golegã,
your celebrated sweets don't tickle my fancy,
no clay cock sings in colour on my shelf,
no lacy whiteness trims my daydreams,
and no banderilla adorns my neck.

Portugal: an ongoing discussion with myself,
a soreness to the bone, an unsated hunger,
a bloodhound on a leash, with no nose and no ducks,
a spruced-up nag,
a dingy fair,
my regret,
my regret for us all...

DOOR TO DOOR

— Who? The infinite?
Tell him to come in!
It's good for infinity
to have human company.

— Our help? He hobbles?
If the fellow's lame,
give him what used to be
Grandfather's cane.

— Dinheiro? Isso não!
Já sei, pobrezinho,
que em vez de pão
ia comprar vinho…

— Teima? Que topete!
Quem se julga ele
se um tigre acabou
nesta sala em tapete?

— Para ir ver a mãe?
Essa é muito forte!
Ele não tem mãe
e não é do Norte…

— Vítima de quê?
O dito está dito.
Se não tinha estofo
quem o mandou ser
infinito?

PERU

Do peru, está tudo dito. Elefante do aviário, o peru não aguenta mais apodos. Podemos, no entanto, garantir que o peru rupe, que não é mau com puré e que, embore prue, morre muito com urpe. O melhor peru é o do vale do Epru. Mas não paga a pena mandá-lo vir de lá. Chegaria a vossas casas sem aquele «repu» que o caracteriza. Podeis, perum, supermercá-lo: vitaminado, vacinado, pesado, congelado, embalado, carimbado, comprovado. Aproveitai, no presente Natal, este superperu, que, para o ano, vendê-lo-ão já mastigado, em bisnagas cheias de préu.

— Some money? No way!
I know the poor swine
instead of bread
would just buy wine.

— He insists? Who on earth
does he take himself for,
when a tiger ended up
as the rug on our floor?

— To go see his mother?
He's putting us on!
He's not from up north,
and his mother's long gone.

— A victim of what?
Look: life is tough.
How can he be infinite
if he's not made of hard
stuff?

TURKEY

Of turkeys, it's all been said. Elephant of the chicken coop, the turkey can't take any more mockery. We can, however, guarantee that the turkey kyrutes, that it isn't bad with sauce, and that, although it's krutey, it dies with much teyruck. The best turkey is from the Urytek valley. But it wouldn't pay to order it from there. It would arrive at your door without that "yutrek" for which it is so famous. You can, truckely, supermarket it: vitaminized, hormonized, sanitized, plasticized, computerized, standardized, justly prized. Take advantage, this very Christmas, of this superturkey which, a year from now, will come pre-chewed, in urkety-filled tubes.

LAMÚRIA DO CEGO QUE ANTES O FOSSE

Quando era cego eu previa
(que freguesia!)
o que ia acontecer.
Era o que se dizia...

Mas agora, que bem vejo,
só agoiro do que vejo
e já ninguém me quer crer...

Porquê,
se todos o podem ver!

PRIMEIRA ADVERTÊNCIA SÉRIA

Coaxa o tempo. Zurra quando calha.
Pipila, o coitadinho. À beira charco,
plofa.

Não te iludas.

Testaruda, a besta arrancará
do meandro de túneis
— para bramir, à luz sem uma prega,
o tempo.

Está atento.

LAMENT OF A MAN WHO MISSES BEING BLIND

When blind, I was famed
(what a lucrative game!)
for being able to tell the future.
So everyone everywhere claimed.

But now that I see perfectly
I use my eyesight to prophesy
and nobody wants to believe me,

since it's plain,
they say, for all to see!

FIRST SERIOUS WARNING

Time creaks. When occasion suits, it brays.
It peeps, poor little thing. At the puddle's edge
it plops.

Don't kid yourself.

Bullheadstrong, the beast tears
from the maze of tunnels
— to bellow forth in broadest noonday blaze
the time.

Beware.

QUERO SABER a madeira
de um nome
a lua das paredes
quero saber quem está vivo
entre vírgulas de terra

Irei ao fundo da sombra
entre apagadas letras
e entre os astros e o mar
abraçarei um arbusto
sobre as águas do verão

Entro num sono lúcido
tão espesso como um fruto
Estou cego e floresço
na cicatriz dos ombros
Ignoro mas conheço
a fluidez essencial

António Ramos Rosa

1924–2012. Born in Faro, the Algarve. Actively involved in a pro-democracy movement in his youth, he was arrested and thrown in jail for three months. Made his living by teaching French and English, writing criticism and translating both in the Algarve and Lisbon, where he settled for good in 1962. From early on his great passion was poetry, and in 1951 he co-founded *Árvore* (1951), a literary magazine that paid considerable attention to international writing. He was especially interested in Paul Éluard and other French poets, and his own poetry has been extensively translated into French.

I WANT TO DISCOVER the wood
of names
the moon of walls
I want to find out who lives
between earthen commas

I'll plumb the shadow
among erased letters
and between stars and sea
I'll embrace a shrub
over the summer's waters

I enter a clear sleep
as heavy as a fruit
Blinded I bloom
in the scar on the shoulders
Ignorant I know
the universal flowing

POR VEZES UM ARVOREDO à nossa volta
e um rio que o atravessa entre ervas altas
é o sítio do mundo em que um estremecimento
desembacia a pupila e desnuda a envergadura
da imóvel tristeza E assim difunde-se
a núbil aragem que é mais do que um prodígio
porque abrindo desenreda a mais obscura trama
e inicia tão fundo e tão por dentro a densidade aberta
que o ser se sente mesmo a nascente do mundo
E estar a ser é como ciência cristalina
que é o saber só da brisa entre a folhagem
e o tremor da água e o ócio fresco
que em círculos crescentes se propaga e renova
Todos seguimos a inclinação clara
e sem demora ardemos de frescura
tão animais do ar como o próprio ar
Iluminam-se as áreas onde é leve
o olvido e o mundo se levanta
sem peso no trânsito do ar
Estendemos as linhas brancas que pensamos
tão rápidas e minuciosas como o vento
e é já real o canto e o grande ritmo
da ignorante inteligência aérea e animal

PERDE-SE COM A IDADE um não sei quê
que era talvez sombra e sabor e até tristeza
e assim temos outra paz de inclinação
em clareiras limpas tocadas de algum eco
melancólico e lúcido E quase sem ilusão
entregamo-nos ao âmbito de uma paz
que é a medida do mundo quando nada
se nos oferece senão o habitar
aquelas horas de um universo que
é no silêncio glória obscura e transparente

SOMETIMES THE MIDDLE of a grove
and next to a river flanked by tall grass
is the place in the world where a shudder
clears our eyes of fog and reveals the breadth
of the immovable sadness That is when the virginal
breeze begins to stir and it is more than a portent
for its unrolling unravels the haziest web
and unlooses such a deep and dense intimacy
that the self feels it is the world's very source
And to be is like a crystalline science
of knowing only the wafting in the foliage
and the tremor of water and its cool quietude
which in widening circles radiates and refreshes
We all follow the sloping path of clarity
and soon find ourselves burning with coolness
as much animals of air as the air itself
Light shines in the patches
where oblivion is wispy and the world
rises weightless through the air's passage
We cast the white lines of our thinking
swift and meticulous as the wind
and already the song and vast rhythm of the ignorant
aerial and animal intelligence are real

WITH AGE WE LOSE I don't know quite what
perhaps shadow and relish and even sadness
and we have a different peace that tends
toward clearings touched by a lucid
melancholy echo And with almost no illusions
we completely surrender to a realm of peace
that is the world's whole extent when nothing
remains but to inhabit the hours
of that universe which in silence
is a darkly transparent glory

Assim nos inebriamos também da madurez
procurando a inocente incandescência
do tempo quando ilumina as clareiras
e é como se nada ainda fosse passado
na onda lenta que ascende sobre o peito
e que desperta um vago núcleo que inicia

PARTIR DOS MINERAIS dos abruptos flancos
ou da lisura dos planos das arestas afiadas
reencontrar a violência da expansão da lava
deixar de ser um ponto de coordenadas
romper os contornos do lugar
quebrar os laços entre o corpo e os seus abrigos
procurar os caminhos sem caminho
onde a sombra se abre como um futuro antigo
Ó coração aberto à terra mais escura
a lâmpada do vazio é a tua bússola
Algo implora talvez o Impossível
Procura tratar as suas feridas negras
com fragmentos de ervas e com pedras
com um pouco de silêncio branco
O que escrevo agora é como um movimento
no fundo do movimento e um tráfego
entre diferentes reinos os vocábulos vibram
com um sangue de silex É aqui
que começa o canto aqui na ausência absoluta
Sou uma árvore de arestas e de nós onde a terra se rasga
sou a paciência magnética da pedra sou o tumulto e o sossego
de um planeta

So that we also get drunk from maturity
looking for the innocent incandescence
of time when it lights up the clearings
and it's as if nothing had yet happened
in the slow wave that swells over the chest
and awakens a hesitant beginning nucleus

START OUT FROM THE MINERALS of steep slopes
or from the smooth planes of whetted edges
rediscover the violence of expanding lava
cease being a point of coordinates
break the surrounding boundaries
cut the ties between the body and its shelters
seek the wayward ways
where shadow opens like an ancient future
O heart that is open to the darkest land
the lamp of emptiness is your compass
Something implores perhaps the Impossible
It tries to heal its black wounds
with scraps of grass and with stones
with a bit of white silence
What I write now is like a movement
in the depths of movement and a commerce
between different kingdoms The words tremble
with a silica blood It is here
that the song begins here in the absolute absence
I am a tree of edges and knots where the earth splits
I am the stone's magnetic patience I am a planet's tumult
        and hush

JÁ NO ENVELHECER se alonga a calma
e no silêncio do fundo o que não é
e unicamente é Qualquer coisa limpa
e harmónica há neste extermínio
que faz cessar a máquina velocíssima
De nada se passar não se passa mais nada?
Não há ninguém no cândido lugar?
Vazia esta morada é viva
e conduz-nos a uma matéria densa
sossegada Pela análise
nada podemos saber mas o prestígio
da sombra escurece-nos e acalma-nos
No íntimo dela não desejamos nada
a não ser que ainda mais se adense o escuro
e na espessura se abra a estranha luz
que é de quem não vê e nâo vendo vê
que nada há para ver e que isso é ver

ONDE ESTOU aqui quisera estar
monotonamente ardente
serenamente vivo
animal da fábula doméstica
concreto sob a materna sombra
fiel ao fundo do tempo
e de mim mesmo

CALMNESS EXTENDS as we get old
along with what in our foundational silence
is not and alone is There is something
clean and harmonious in the extermination
that brings this rapid machine to a halt
Does nothing now happening mean nothing else will?
Is there no one in the place of innocence?
Vacant this abode is alive
and leads us to a peaceful
dense matter We can know nothing
by way of analysis but the spell
of the shadow darkens and calms us
Inside it there is nothing we desire
except that the darkness would grow yet thicker
and the density give way to the strange light
of one who doesn't see and not seeing sees
that there is nothing to see and that this is seeing

WHERE I AM here I want to be
monotonously ardent
serenely alive
an animal of the domestic fable
concrete under the maternal shadow
faithful to deep time
and to my deepest self

PREFÁCIO

Falemos de casas, do sagaz exercício de um poder
tão firme e silencioso como só houve
no tempo mais antigo.
Estes são os arquitectos, aqueles que vão morrer,
sorrindo com ironia e doçura no fundo
de um alto segredo que os restitui à lama.
De doces mãos irreprimíveis.
— Sobre os meses, sonhando nas últimas chuvas,
as casas encontram seu inocente jeito de durar contra
a boca subtil rodeada em cima pela treva das palavras.

Digamos que descobrimos amoras, a corrente oculta
do gosto, o entusiasmo do mundo.
Descobrimos corpos de gente que se protege e sorve, e o silêncio
admirável das fontes —
pensamentos nas pedras de alguma coisa celeste
como fogo exemplar.

Herberto Helder

Born in 1930, in Funchal, Madeira. Studied first law, then literature, at the University of Coimbra, without earning a degree. Held a wide variety of jobs in Lisbon, in Madeira, and in France, Belgium and the Netherlands. Spent most of the 1960s in Lisbon, where he worked for a few years as a radio journalist. Went to Angola in 1971 to be a magazine reporter. Returned to Lisbon before the 25 April 1974 revolution and worked once more in radio as well as for magazines. Gradually became more reclusive, shunning publicity and refusing to give interviews or accept prizes. As a young man he met regularly with Mário Cesariny and other poets and intellectuals in cafés, and he edited or participated in various publications of experimental poetry.

PREFACE

I want to speak of houses, and of the sages
who wield that solid and silent
power hailing from ancient times.
I mean the architects, the ones who are going to die
smiling with sweet irony in the depths
of a sublime secret that returns them to mud.
With soft irrepressible hands.
— Across the months, dreaming of the last rains,
the houses discover their innocent knack for enduring against
the mouth that lurks under the whirling chaos of words.

Say we discover blackberries, the occult current
of taste, the world's enthusiasm.
Say we discover bodies of self-protected, withdrawn people, and the stunning
silence of fountains —
thoughts in stones about something celestial
like exemplary fire.

Digamos que dormimos nas casas, e vemos as musas
um pouco inclinadas para nós como estreitas e erguidas flores
tenebrosas, e temos memória
e absorvente melancolia
e atenção às portas sobre a extinção dos dias altos.

Estas são as casas. E se vamos morrer nós mesmos,
espantamo-nos um pouco, e muito, com tais arquitectos
que não viram as torrentes infindáveis
das rosas, ou as águas permanentes,
ou um sinal de eternidade espalhado nos corações
rápidos.
— Que fizeram estes arquitectos destas casas, eles que vagabundearam
pelos muitos sentidos dos meses,
dizendo: aqui fica uma casa, aqui outra, aqui outra,
para que se faça uma ordem, uma duração,
uma beleza contra a força divina?

Alguém trouxera cavalos, descendo os caminhos da montanha.
Alguém viera do mar.
Alguém chegara do estrangeiro, coberto de pó.
Alguém lera livros, poemas, profecias, mandamentos,
inspirações.
— Estas casas serão destruídas.
Como um girassol, elaborado para a bebedeira, insistente
no seu casamento solar, assim
se esgotará cada casa, esbulhada de um fogo,
vergando a demorada cabeça para os rios misteriosos
da terra
onde os próprios arquitectos se desfazem com suas mãos
múltiplas, as caras ardendo nas velozes
iluminações.

Falemos de casas. É verão, outono,
nome profuso entre as paisagens inclinadas
Traziam o sal, os construtores
da alma, comportavam em si

Say we sleep in the houses, and see the muses
gently leaning over us like gloomy flowers,
tall and slender, and we remember
and are melancholy
and watch the doors close on the demise of the lofty days.

These are the houses. And knowing that we ourselves will die,
we wonder a little, and a lot, at those architects
who did not see the endless torrents
of roses, or the unceasing waters,
or a sign of eternity scattered in quick-beating
hearts.
— What did the architects of these houses do as they roamed
through the months' many directions,
saying one house goes here, one there, another over there,
to make for some order, a duration,
a beauty against the divine force?

Someone brought horses, coming down the mountain paths.
Someone came from the sea.
Someone came from abroad, all covered with dust.
Someone read books, poems, prophecies, commandments,
inspirations.
— These houses will be destroyed.
Like a sunflower, fashioned for drunkenness, insisting
on its solar wedding, so each house
will wither away, bereft of a fire,
bowing its sluggish head toward the mysterious rivers
of the earth
where the architects themselves will disintegrate by their own
multiple hands, their faces burning in the swift
illuminations.

I want to speak of houses. It is summer, autumn,
the name bursting over sloping landscapes.
The builders of the soul brought
salt, carrying in themselves a restorative awe

restituidores deslumbramentos em presença da suspensão
de animais e estrelas,
imaginavam bem a pureza com homens e mulheres
ao lado uns dos outros, sorrindo enigmaticamente,
tocando uns nos outros —
comovidos, difíceis, dadivosos,
ardendo devagar.

Só um instante em cada primavera se encontravam
com o junquilho original,
arrefeciam o resto do ano, eram breves os mestres
da inspiração.
— E as casas levantavam-se
sobre as águas ao comprido do céu.
Mas casas, arquitectos, encantadas trocas de carne
doce e obsessiva — tudo isso
está longe da canção que era preciso escrever.

— E de tudo os espelhos são a invenção mais impura.

Falemos de casas, da morte. Casas são rosas
para cheirar muito cedo, ou à noite, quando a esperança
nos abandona para sempre.
Casas são rios diuturnos, nocturnos rios
celestes que fulguram lentamente
até uma baía fria — que talvez não exista,
como uma secreta eternidade.

Falemos de casas como quem fala da sua alma,
entre um incêndio,
junto ao modelo das searas,
na aprendizagem da paciência de vê-las erguer
e morrer com um pouco, um pouco
de beleza.

before the sight of suspended
animals and stars,
and they conceived of purity, with men and women
side by side, smiling enigmatically,
touching each other —
tender, diffident, inclined to give,
timidly burning.

For a fleeting moment each spring they met
with the first and original jonquil,
turning cool for the rest of the year, so brief were the masters
of inspiration.
— And the houses rose up
over the waters all across the sky.
But houses, architects and enchanted exchanges
of sweet, obsessive flesh — none of this went
into the song that needed to be written.

— And mirrors are the impurest invention of all.

I want to speak of houses, of death. Houses are roses
to be smelled early in the day, or at night, when hope
abandons us forever.
Houses are nocturnal, enduring, celestial
rivers that slowly shimmer
toward a cold bay — which perhaps does not exist,
like a secret eternity.

I want to speak of houses as a man speaks of his soul,
in the midst of a fire,
next to the example of the wheat fields,
learning the patience that watches them rise
and die with a hint, a hint
of beauty.

«TRANSFORMA-SE O AMADOR na coisa amada» com seu
feroz sorriso, os dentes,
as mãos que relampejam no escuro. Traz ruído
e silêncio. Traz o barulho das ondas frias
e das ardentes pedras que tem dentro de si.
E cobre esse ruído rudimentar com o assombrado
silêncio da sua última vida.
O amador transforma-se de instante para instante,
e sente-se o espírito imortal do amor
criando a carne em extremas atmosferas, acima
de todas as coisas mortas.

Transforma-se o amador. Corre pelas formas dentro.
E a coisa amada é uma baía estanque.
É o espaço de um castiçal,
a coluna vertebral e o espírito
das mulheres sentadas.
Transforma-se em noite extintora.
Porque o amador é tudo, e a coisa amada
é uma cortina
onde o vento do amador bate no alto da janela
aberta. O amador entra
por todas as janelas abertas. Ele bate, bate, bate.
O amador é um martelo que esmaga.
Que transforma a coisa amada.

Ele entra pelos ouvidos, e depois a mulher
que escuta
fica com aquele grito para sempre na cabeça
a arder como o primeiro dia do verão. Ela ouve
e vai-se transformando, enquanto dorme, naquele grito
do amador.
Depois acorda, e vai, e dá-se ao amador,
dá-lhe o grito dele.
E o amador e a coisa amada são um único grito
anterior de amor.

"THE LOVER TRANSFORMS into the thing loved" with his
savage smile, his teeth,
his hands that flash in the dark. He brings sound
and silence. Brings the noise of the cold waves breaking
and the stones burning inside him.
And he covers this primordial sound with the staggered
silence of his last life.
The lover transforms from moment to moment,
and it's the moment of the immortal spirit of love
creating flesh in extreme atmospheres, wafting
over all dead things.

The lover transforms. Cuts through forms to the core.
And the thing loved is an enclosed bay,
the space of a candlestick,
the backbone and spirit
of women sitting.
He transforms into extinguishing night,
Because the lover is everything, and the thing loved
is a curtain
battered by the wind of the lover on the heights
of an open window. The lover enters
through every open window and batters, batters, batters.
The lover is a smashing hammer.
That transforms the thing loved.

He enters through her ears, and the woman
who listens
holds that shout forever in her mind
burning like the first day of summer. She hears
and slowly transforms, while sleeping, into that shout
of the lover.
She awakens, and goes, and gives herself to the lover,
she gives him his own shout.
And the lover and the thing loved are a single shout
preceding love.

E gritam e batem. Ele bate-lhe com o seu espírito
de amador. E ela é batida, e bate-lhe
com o seu espírito de amada.
Então o mundo transforma-se neste ruído áspero
do amor. Enquanto em cima
o silêncio do amador e da amada alimentam
o imprevisto silêncio do mundo
e do amor.

TEORIA SENTADA (II)

Alguém parte uma laranja em silêncio, à entrada
de noites fabulosas.
Mergulha os polegares até onde a laranja
pensa velozmente, e se desenvolve, e aniquila, e depois
renasce. Alguém descasca uma pêra, come
um bago de uva, devota-se
aos frutos. E eu faço uma canção arguta
para entender.
Inclino-me para as mãos ocupadas, as bocas,
as línguas que devoram pela atenção dentro.
Eu queria saber como se acrescenta assim
a fábula das noites. Como o silêncio
se engrandece, ou se transforma com as coisas. Escrevo
uma canção para ser inteligente dos frutos
na língua, por canais subtis, até
uma emoção escura.

Porque o amor também recolhe as cascas
e o mover dos dedos
e a suspensão da boca sobre o gosto
confuso. Também o amor se coloca às portas
das noites ferozes
e procura entender como elas imaginam seu
poder estrangeiro.

And they shout and batter. He batters her with his lover
spirit. And she is battered and batters him
with her spirit of the beloved.
Then the world transforms into this harsh noise
of love. While overhead
the silence of the lover and the beloved feed
the surprising silence of the world
and of love.

SEATED THEORY (II)

Someone breaks an orange in silence, on the threshold
of fabulous nights,
thumbs plunging to where the orange
swiftly thinks, and develops, and annihilates, and then
is reborn. Someone peels a pear, eats
a grape, is devoted
to fruits. And I write a shrewd song
to understand.
I lean over the busy hands, the mouths,
the tongues that devour with penetrating attention.
I want to learn how this makes
the fable of nights grow. How silence
enlarges or transforms with things. I write
a song to have knowledge about fruits
on the tongue, in subtle canals, down
to a dark emotion.

Because love also gathers the peels
and the fingers' movement
and the mouth's stupor when bombarded
by taste. Love also stands at the doors
of wild nights
and tries to understand how they imagine their
foreign power.

Aniquilar os frutos para saber, contra
a paixão do gosto, que a terra trabalha a sua
solidão — é devotar-se,
esgotar a amada, para ver como o amor
trabalha na sua loucura.
Uma canção de agora dirá que as noites
esmagam
o coração. Dirá que o amor aproxima
a eternidade, ou que o gosto
revela os ritmos diuturnos, os segredos
da escuridão.
Porque é com nomes que alguém sabe
onde estar um corpo
por uma ideia, onde um pensamento
faz a vez da língua.
— É com as vozes que o silêncio ganha.

JÁ NÃO TENHO TEMPO para ganhar o amor, a glória ou a Abissínia,
talvez me reste um tiro na cabeça,
e é tão cinematográfico e tão sem número o número dos efeitos especiais,
mas não quero complicar coisas tão simples da terra,
bom seria entrar no sono como num saco maior que o meu tamanho,
e que uns dedos inexplicáveis lhe dessem um nó rude,
e eu de dentro o não pudesse desfazer:
um saco sem qualquer explicação,
que ficasse para ali num sítio ele mesmo sítio bem amarrado
— não um destino à Rimbaud,
apenas longe, sem barras de ouro, sem amputação de pernas,
esquecido de mim mesmo num saco atado cegamente,
num recanto pela idade fora,
e lá dentro os dias eram à noite bem no fundo,
um saco sem qualquer salvação nos armazéns confusos

Annihilating fruits to discover, against
the passion of taste, that the earth works its
solitude — it is devotion,
wearing out the beloved, to see how love
works in its madness.
A song of this moment will say that these nights
overwhelm
the heart. It will say that love comes close
to eternity, or that taste
reveals the enduring rhythms, the secrets
of darkness.
For it is with names that we know
where to posit a body
for an idea, where a thought
takes the place of the tongue.
— It is with voices that silence prevails.

IT'S TOO LATE FOR LOVE, glory or Abyssinia,
at this point perhaps all I can manage is a shot in the head,
just like in the movies and with an innumerable number of special
effects,
but I'd rather not complicate such simple earthly matters,
I'd like to slip into sleep as into a sack bigger than me,
a sack that inexplicable fingers would tie shut with a quick knot
I couldn't undo from inside,
a sack without any explanation,
tied up and left there in some place itself the place
— not a destiny à la Rimbaud,
just far away, without gold bars, without amputated legs,
oblivious to my own self in a tightly tied up sack,
in a corner beyond all years,
and inside it the days would pass at night in the depths,
a sack in the murky warehouses with no salvation

E TUDO ERA POSSÍVEL

Na minha juventude antes de ter saído
da casa de meus pais disposto a viajar
eu conhecia já o rebentar do mar
das páginas dos livros que já tinha lido

Chegava o mês de maio era tudo florido
o rolo das manhãs punha-se a circular
e era só ouvir o sonhador falar
da vida como se ela houvesse acontecido

E tudo se passava numa outra vida
e havia para as coisas sempre uma saída
Quando foi isso? Eu próprio não o sei dizer

Só sei que tinha o poder duma criança
entre as coisas e mim havia vizinhança
e tudo era possível era só querer

Ruy Belo

1933–1978. Born in São João da Ribeira, a small town in central Portugal. Earned a law degree at the University of Lisbon and a PhD in Canonical Law at the Gregorian University of Rome. Joined Opus Dei in 1951 but quit the organization in 1961, the same year he published his first book of poems and began to pursue a degree in Romance Languages and Literature, again at the University of Lisbon. Lecturer of Portuguese in Madrid between 1971 and 1977. Because of his public opposition to the Salazar regime, he was unable to secure a position at a Portuguese university. Translator from the French and Spanish.

AND EVERYTHING WAS POSSIBLE

When I was still young before I left home
all eager to travel around the world
I already knew about the waves' breaking
from the pages of all the books I'd read

When May rolled around everything was flowers
the morning turtledove flew here flew there
and to hear the dreamer just speak of life
was like having it actually happen

Everything took place in another life
and there was always a way out when needed
When was all of this? Not even I know

I know only that I had a child's power
all things were close to me and everything
was possible I only had to want it

PEREGRINO E HÓSPEDE SOBRE A TERRA

Meu único país é sempre onde estou bem
é onde pago o bem com sofrimento
é onde num momento tudo tenho
O meu país agora são os mesmos campos verdes
que no outono vi tristes e desolados
e onde nem me pedem passaporte
pois neles nasci e morro a cada instante
que a paz não é palavra para mim
O malmequer a erva o pessegueiro em flor
asseguram o mínimo de dor indispensável
a quem na felicidade que tivesse
veria uma reforma e um insulto
A vida recomeça e o sol brilha
a tudo isto chamam primavera
mas nada disto cabe numa só palavra
abstrata quando tudo é tão concreto e vário
O meu país são todos os amigos
que conquisto e que perco a cada instante
Os meus amigos são os mais recentes
os dos demais países os que mal conheço e
tenho de abandonar porque me vou embora
pois eu nunca estou bem aonde estou
nem mesmo estou sequer aonde estou
Eu não sou muito grande nasci numa aldeia
mas o país que tinha já de si pequeno
fizeram-no pequeno para mim
os donos das pessoas e das terras
os vendilhões das almas no templo do mundo
Sou donde estou e só sou português
por ter em portugal olhado a luz pela primeira vez

PILGRIM AND GUEST ON PLANET EARTH

My only country is where I feel at home
it's where I pay for that feeling with suffering
it's where in an instant I have everything
Right now my country is the same green fields
which looked sad and forlorn to me in autumn
and where I never need to show a passport
since that's where I was born and at each moment die
peace not being a word that applies to me
The daisy the grass the peach tree in flower
guarantee the minimum of necessary pain
for a man who would look upon any happiness
as a pension check or an insult
Life begins anew the sun is shining
and this is called spring
but it's far too varied and concrete
to fit into just one abstract word
My country is all the friends
I keep making and losing
My friends are the most recent ones
those from other countries those I hardly know and
I have to leave them because I'm going away
since I'm never at home where I am
I'm not even here where I am
I'm not very big I was born in a village
and my country that was small to begin with
became even smaller for me
owing to the landowners and people-owners
and the hawkers of souls in the temple of the world
I'm me where I am and I'm only portuguese
for having first seen light in portugal

OH AS CASAS AS CASAS AS CASAS

Oh as casas as casas as casas
as casas nascem vivem e morrem
Enquanto vivas distinguem-se umas das outras
distinguem-se designadamente pelo cheiro
variam até de sala pra sala
As casas que eu fazia em pequeno
onde estarei eu hoje em pequeno?
Onde estarei aliás eu dos versos daqui a pouco?
Terei eu casa onde reter tudo isto
ou serei sempre somente esta instabilidade?
As casas essas parecem estáveis
mas são tão frágeis as pobres casas
Oh as casas as casas as casas
mudas testemunhas da vida
elas morrem não só ao ser demolidas
elas morrem com a morte das pessoas
As casas de fora olham-nos pelas janelas
Não sabem nada de casas os construtores
os senhorios os procuradores
Os ricos vivem nos seus palácios
mas a casa dos pobres é todo o mundo
os pobres sim têm o conhecimento das casas
os pobres esses conhecem tudo
Eu amei as casas os recantos das casas
Visitei casas apalpei casas
Só as casas explicam que exista
uma palavra como intimidade
Sem casas não haveria ruas
as ruas onde passamos pelos outros
mas passamos principalmente por nós
Na casa nasci e hei-de morrer
na casa sofri convivi amei
na casa atravessei as estações
respirei — ó vida simples problema de respiração
Oh as casas as casas as casas

OH HOUSES HOUSES HOUSES

Oh houses houses houses
houses are born they live they die
While alive they stand out from each other
they stand out namely by their smell
they differ even from room to room
The houses I built in my childhood
where am I today in my childhood?
And where will the I of my verses be later on?
Will I have a house where I can keep all of this
or will I always be just this instability?
Unlike me houses seem stable
but they're so fragile poor houses
Oh houses houses houses
silent witnesses of life
they die not only when demolished
they die with the death of people
Houses look outside their windows at us
Builders landlords and real estate agents
know nothing about houses
Rich people have their palaces
but the house of the poor is the whole world
it's the poor who know about houses
the poor know everything
I've loved houses their nooks and corners
I've visited houses fondled houses
Only houses can explain
why a word like intimacy exists
Without houses there would be no streets
the streets where we cross paths with others
and especially with ourselves
In a house I was born and I'll die
in a house I suffered I lived with others I loved
in a house I went through the seasons
I breathed — O life simple matter of breathing
Oh houses houses houses

REQUIEM POR UM CÃO

Cão que matinalmente farejavas a calçada
as ervas os calhaus os seixos e os paralelepípedos
os restos de comida os restos de manhã
a chuva antes caída e convertida numa como que auréola da terra
cão que isso farejavas cão que nada disso já farejas
Foi um segundo súbito e ficaste ensanduichado
esborrachado comprimido e reduzido
debaixo do rodado imperturbável do pesado camião
Que tinhas que não tens diz-mo ou ladra-mo
ou utiliza então qualquer moderno meio de comunicação
diz-me lá cão que faísca fugiu do teu olhar
que falta nesse corpo afinal o mesmo corpo
só que embalado ou liofilizado?
Eras vivo e morreste nada mais teus donos
se é que os tinhas sempre que de ti falavam
falavam no presente falam no passado agora
Mudou alguma coisa de um momento para o outro
coisa sem importância de maior para quem passa
indiferente até ao halo da manhã de pensamento posto
em coisas práticas em coisas próximas
Cão que morreste tão caninamente
cão que morreste e me fazes pensar parar até
que o polícia me diz que siga em frente
Que se passou então? um simples cão que era e já não é

RELATÓRIO E CONTAS

Setembro é o teu mês, homem da tarde
anunciada em folhas como uma ameaça
Ninguém morreu ainda e tudo treme já
Ventos e chuvas rondam pelos côncavos dos céus
e brilhas como quem no próprio brilho se consome
Tens retiradas hábeis, sabes como

REQUIEM FOR A DOG

Dog that each morning sniffed the street
the grass the pebbles gravel and paving stones
the scraps of food the scraps of morning
the fallen rain converted into a kind of halo for the earth
dog that sniffed all of this dog that sniffs none of this
It took but a second for you to be sandwiched
squeezed squashed and flattened
by the unfeeling wheels of a massive truck
Tell me or bark at me what you had and now don't have
or use some modern means of communication
to explain dog what spark disappeared from your eyes
what's missing from your body still the very same body
just packed up or freeze-dried
You were alive and you died that's all and your owners
if you had any always talked when they talked of you
in the present now they'll talk in the past
Something changed from one moment to the next
something of scant importance for those who pass by
oblivious even to the morning's halo their minds focused
on practical things on upcoming things
dog that died so doggishly
dog that died and that makes me think of stopping until
the policeman tells me to keep on moving
So what happened? A dog just a dog that was and now isn't

RECKONING AND REPORT

September is your month, man of day's end
announced in leaves like a warning
No one has died and yet everything's trembling
Winds and rains whirl in the sky's hollows
and you glow as if self-consumed in your glowing
You know when to retreat, you know how the apple

a maçã se arredonda e se rebola à volta do que a rói
Há uvas há o trigo e o búzio da azeitona asperge em leque o som inabalável
nos leves ondulados e restritos renques das mais longínquas oliveiras conhecidas
Poisas sólidos pés sobre tantas traições e no entanto foste jovem
e tinhas quem sinceramente acreditasse em ti
A consciência mói-te mais que uma doença
reúnes em redor da casa equilibrada restos de rebanhos
e voltas entre estevas pelos múltiplos caminhos
Há fumos névoas noites coisas que se elevam e dispersam
regressas como quem dependurado cai da sua podridão de pomo
Reconheces o teu terrível nome as rugas do teu riso
começam já então a retalhar-te a cara
Despedias poentes por diversos pontos realmente
És aquele que no maior número possível de palavras nada disse
Comprazes-te contigo quando o próprio sol
desce sobre o teu pátio e passa tantas mãos na pele dos rostos que tiveste
Repara: não esbarras já contra a cor amarela?
Setembro na verdade é mês para voltar
Podes tentar ainda alguns expedientes respeitáveis
multiplicar diversas diligências nos ameaçados cumes dos outeiros
ser e não ser fugir do rótulo aceitar e esquivar o nome fixo
E no entanto é inevitável: a temperatura descerá mais dia menos dia
Calas-te então cumprido como um rosto e puxas toda a tarde
sobre esse corpo que se estende e jaz
Andaste de lugar para lugar e deste o dito por não dito
mas todos toda a vida teus credores saberão onde encontrar-te
pois passarás a estar nalguma parte
Tens domicílio ali que a terra sobe levemente
e toda a tua boca ambiciosa sabe e sente quanto barro encerra

A MÃO NO ARADO

Feliz aquele que administra sabiamente
a tristeza e aprende a reparti-la pelos dias
Podem passar os meses e os anos nunca lhe faltará

grows round and wraps around what gnaws it
There are grapes there's wheat and the olive horn sprinkles its unfailing sound
all over the neat and weightless waving rows of the farthest olive trees known
Your solid feet tread over countless treacheries but once you were young
and knew people who sincerely believed in you
Conscience eats at you more than any disease
you gather your remaining sheep around your well-ordered house
and go back by the multiple paths weaving through rockroses
There are mists smoke nights things that rise and scatter
you return like someone who dangling falls from his applish rottenness
You recognize your awful name the wrinkles born of laughter
are already beginning to furrow your face
You indeed waved farewell to sunsets in various places
You're the one who in the greatest number of words possible said nothing
You delight in yourself when the brilliant sun
falls on your patio and runs myriad hands over the skin of all the faces you've had
Watch out: aren't you verging already on the colour yellow?
September is in truth a month for going back
You can still attempt some respectable expedients
multiply your efforts on the threatened summits of hills
be and not be dodge all labels accept and elude fixed names
And yet it's inevitable: the temperature will drop sooner or later
Then you'll fall silent your duty as a face all done and you'll pull the whole
afternoon
over your stretched out body that lies stock-still
You went from place to place and denied here what you said there
but your life's long line of creditors will know where to find you
since you'll end up being somewhere
You have a domicile right there where the earth slightly rises
and your ambitious mouth knows and feels how much dirt it can hold

HAND TO THE PLOUGH

Happy the man who manages sadness wisely
and learns to divide it among the days
Though months and years pass it will never leave him

Oh! como é triste envelhecer à porta
entretecer nas mãos um coração tardio
Oh! como é triste arriscar em humanos regressos
o equilíbrio azul das extremas manhãs do verão
ao longo do mar transbordante de nós
no demorado adeus da nossa condição
É triste no jardim a solidão do sol
vê-lo desde o rumor e as casas da cidade
até uma vaga promessa de rio
e a pequenina vida que se concede às unhas
Mais triste é termos de nascer e morrer
e haver árvores ao fim da rua

É triste ir pela vida como quem
regressa e entrar humildemente por engano pela morte dentro
É triste no outono concluir
que era o verão a única estação
Passou o solidário vento e não o conhecemos
e não soubemos ir até ao fundo da verdura
como rios que sabem onde encontrar o mar
e com que pontes com que ruas com que gentes com que montes
conviver
através de palavras de uma água para sempre dita
Mas o mais triste é recordar os gestos de amanhã

Triste é comprar castanhas depois da tourada
entre o fumo e o domingo na tarde de novembro
e ter como futuro o asfalto e muita gente
e atrás a vida sem nenhuma infância
revendo tudo isto algum tempo depois
A tarde morre pelos dias fora
É muito triste andar por entre Deus ausente

Mas, ó poeta, administra a tristeza sabiamente

How sad it is to grow old on the doorstep
while weaving in our hands a belated heart
How sad to risk against human returns
the blue equilibrium of summer's sheer mornings
by the ocean that overflows with us
in the long farewell of our condition
It is sad to see in the garden the sun's solitude
reaching from the city's houses and din
to a distant hint of river
and the meagre life meted out to us
It is sadder to have to be born and to die
and to have trees at the end of the street

It is sad to go through life as if
returning and to humbly enter death by mistake
It is sad in autumn to conclude that summer
was the only season
The wind passed by in solidarity and we didn't see it
and we didn't know to go to the green depths
like rivers that know where to find the sea
conversing on the way with this bridge that street these people
those hills
through the words of a forever uttered water
But what's saddest is to remember tomorrow's acts

It is sad to buy roasted chestnuts after the bullfight
amid the smoke on a sunday afternoon in november
and to have asphalt and many people for your future
and behind you a life with no childhood
looking back at all of this some time later
Day by day the afternoon dies
It is very sad to walk among God and be absent

But manage, poet, your sadness wisely

NATUREZA MORTA COM LOUVADEUS

Foi o último hóspede a sentar-se
no topo da mesa, já depois do martírio.
As asas magníficas haviam-lhe sido quebradas
por algum vento. Perdera o rumo
sobre a película cintilante de água
no riacho parado. Tal como poisou
junto de nós, com o belo corpo magro
arquejante, lembrava, ainda segundo o seu nome,
um santo mártir. Enquanto meditávamos,
a morte sobreveio, e a pequena criatura,
que viera partilhar a nossa mesa,
depois de ter sido banida das águas
foi banida da terra. Alguém pegou
no volúvel alado corpo morto
abandonado sem nexo na brancura da toalha
— que maculava —

Fiama Hasse Pais Brandão

1938–2007. Born in Lisbon. Earned a degree in Germanic Languages and Literature at the University of Lisbon, where she co-founded a student theatre group. Began publishing at the age of 19, but *Morfismos* — a chapbook published in the magazine *Poesia 61* — was the first poetry title she included in her collected poetry. Active in theatre as a playwright and in other capacities.

STILL-LIFE WITH PRAYING MANTIS

He was the last guest to seat himself
upon the table-top, just after martyrdom.
His magnificent wings had been broken
by the wind. He had lost his way
along the glittering film of water
in the stagnant ditch. The way he settled
next to us, with his beautiful thin body
gasping, made one think, in accordance with his name,
of a martyred saint. While we pondered,
death descended, and the small creature,
who had come to share our meal,
having been banished from the waters
now was banished from the earth. Someone picked up
the whimsical winged body
abandoned, dead and disconnected on the whiteness of the tablecloth
— which it was staining —

e o atirou para qualquer arbusto raro
que o poeta ainda pôde fotografar.

LOUVOR DO GAFANHOTO

Tantas vezes na mão o coração senti
ao estrebuchar entre os meus dedos
o gafanhoto incauto. Prender
as finas pautas num ângulo.
O tudo e o nada consubstanciados
neste ser que imita o tronco seco
e quer ser nada ou o não ser.
Que deixa a mão do cenobita
trémula segui-lo e humilimamente
é todo o seu alimento.

ESCREVO COMO UM ANIMAL, mas com menor
perfeição alucinatória. Não sei imprimir as três linhas
convergentes do pé da gaivota, nem os pomos
leves da pata dos felinos. Só de uma forma rudimentar
escrevo, e estou a predestinar-me ao fim.
Depois de tantos séculos posso afirmar
que a escrita é uma escravidão dura.
Sei que é inútil e desumano mover as mãos
assim. Nem estou convicta de que seja digno
escrever desta maneira; é uma manufactura triste,
quando as mãos podiam apenas escarvar
na terra ou no corpo. Podem ficar as palavras
somente na fita magnética como nas cabeças loiras.
Nada na infância nos deveria obrigar
a traçar as patas dos roedores repelentes

and threw it into some rare shrub
where the poet still could take a photograph.

IN PRAISE OF THE LOCUST

How often have I felt in my hand,
between my fingers, the heart
of the careless locust. Grasping
the delicate feet at an angle.
The all and nothingness consubstantial
in this being who imitates a dry trunk
and wishes to be nothing or non-being itself.
Who allows the hand of the cenobite,
trembling, to follow him and, in plain humility,
is all the food he has to eat.

I WRITE LIKE AN ANIMAL, but with less
hallucinatory perfection. I don't know how to leave the print of three
convergent lines on a sea gull's foot or the light
pad of a feline's paw. I can only write in a rudimentary
way, predestining myself to my end.
After so many centuries, I can affirm
that writing is a hard enslavement.
I know that it is futile and inhuman to move my hands
like this. Nor am I convinced that it is dignified
to write this way; it's a sad handicraft,
when the hands can only scratch the surface
of the earth or of a body. Words could just as well
stay on a tape or inside blond heads.
Nothing in childhood should have forced us
to trace out those disgusting rodent paws,

que são letras. O som da boca deve escrever-se
no écran, com a nova razão da nova máquina
da realidade. Na areia, porém, ou no mosaico molhado
terei de aperfeiçoar a minha pegada. Aproximar
dela a mão até alcançar a harmonia do trilho
do escaravelho. Uma fieira de montículos
e ranhuras até ao infinito que para ele é o mar.
Há quantos séculos os seres humanos me aprisionaram
no mito da caligrafia. Como tem sido penoso esse gesto,
há tanto tempo, e só eu o renego, porque sinto
a opressão com que alguém o tornou mais nobre
do que a minha fala ou a minha visão, únicas
propensões inatas. Prefiro aprender pormenorizadamente
a conservar uma impressão digital. Há um pensamento
abstracto e maquinal que decora a História com inteligência
mecânica, e por isso é supérfluo escrever. Só alguns
raros escribas, como os desenhadores de máquinas,
seriam necessários. E poderia descansar a cabeça
no regaço da lama.

Ensinaria à infância a gravar
no pó de talco a palma das mãos e a considerar as palavras
modulações da voz pura, sem a mancha embaciada
compacta que paira diante dos olhos sempre
que se fala. A mancha que se desloca no raio de visão
e desbota qualquer imagem como a chama de uma vela
com a fuligem constante a torná-la opaca.

FURO O CHÃO para dar passagem
à toupeira. Ela ascende. Dança com
o fogo. Dou aos animais as vivências
que me sobejam. Reparto com Eurípedes
o pão. Uma parte do todo pertence ao poema
outra à minha voragem. O charco

the letters of the alphabet. The sound of the mouth ought to be
written
on a screen, with the new reasoning of the new machine
of reality. It's in the sand, however, or on wet tiles
that I will have to hone my tracks. To extend my
hand toward it, till I reach the harmony of the
beetle's path. A row of tiny hillocks
and gullies, leading to the infinite, which for it is the sea.
For how many centuries has humankind imprisoned me
in the myth of calligraphy! As if this gesture had turned to pain,
so long ago, and I alone renounce it, for I feel
the oppression with which someone has turned it more noble
than my speech or my seeing, my only
innate propensities. I'd rather learn in detail
how to preserve a fingerprint. There is an abstract
and mechanical thought that memorizes History with mechanical
intelligence, therefore it is superfluous to write. Only a few
rare scribes, like designers of machines,
would be needed. And I could rest my head
in a lap of mud.

I would teach children to engrave
their palms in talcum powder and to consider words
modulations of pure voice, without that thick and tarnished
stain that hovers before one's eyes whenever
one speaks. A stain that moves within the field of vision
and smudges every image like the flame of a candle,
its endless soot turning it opaque.

I BORE THROUGH THE GROUND to make way
for the mole. It climbs up. It dances
with fire. I give the remainder of my experiences
to animals. I break bread with
Euripides. One part of everything belongs to the poem,
the other to my voracity. The stagnant pool

refresca-me. Está presente. Oscilo
entre o cénico e o lírico. As coisas
que me rodeiam são. Cada uma prepara
a sua transformação. A abstracção que está
próxima da abstracção. Um cansaço apaga-as.

O fôlego dos poemas esgota-se.
As pontas das chamas chiam.
Aqui nós somos existentes. Quem passa
no ar. Tiras de nuvens
carbonizadas. Horizonte onde Bóreas
ainda está.

CANTO DO GÉNESIS

Ao princípio era a luz, depois o céu
azul porque a luz se embebe
nas camadas de ar que olhamos.
Ao princípio era a Paixão e engendrou
do seu sangue os animais, da sua
Cruz as plantas. Era, ao princípio,
o animal-vegetal minúsculo, oculto
no Paraíso, mas omnipresente
desde o ante-princípio. E da argila
ou terra adâmica formou-se a Natureza
e o Homem, banhados pela luz
que recortou linhas e volumes vagos.
Ao princípio era o martírio
e a bênção daquele que trabalha
o seu corpo e o seu pão de sol a sol.
E os frutos fulguraram nessa luz
quando as águas se apartaram
e o mar, até hoje, quebra e requebra a onda
para eu ouvir o som do início.

refreshes me. It is present. I waver
between the scenic and the lyric. The things
that surround me are. Each one preparing
its transformation. The abstracted that is
next to abstraction. Exhaustion snuffs them out.

The breath of the poems is spent.
The tips of the flames sizzle.
Here we are, existing. Passing
through the air. Ribbons of carbonized
clouds. A horizon where Boreas
still remains.

SONG OF GENESIS

In the beginning there was light, then
blue sky, because light is absorbed
in the layers of air we see.
In the beginning was the Passion, and from
its blood sprang the animals, from its
Cross the plants. There was, in the beginning,
the tiny vegetable-animal, hidden
in Paradise but omnipresent
since before the beginning. And the Edenic
earth or clay gave substance to Nature
and Man, bathed by the light
which sculpted lines and hazy shapes.
In the beginning there was the sweat
and blessing of those who work
their body and their bread from sun to sun.
And the fruits gleamed in that light
when the waters separated, and the sea,
to this day, breaks its waves without ceasing
so that I can hear the sound of genesis.

CANTO DOS LUGARES

Tantas vezes os lugares habitam no Homem
e os homens tantas vezes habitam
nos lugares que os habitam, que podia
dizer-se que o cárcere de Socrates,
estando nele Socrates, não o era,
como diz Seneca em epístola a Helvia.

Por isso cada lugar nos mostra
uma vida clara e desmedida,
enquanto o Tempo oscila e nos oculta
que é curto e ambíguo
porque nos dá a morte e a vida.

E os lugares somente acabam
porque é mortal cada homem
que houve em si algum lugar.

SONG OF PLACES

Since places so often live in Man
and men so often live in places
that live in them, we can say
that Socrates' jail, since Socrates
was in it, was not a jail,
as Seneca said in a letter to Helvia.

And so each place shows us
a clear and boundless life, while Time
goes back and forth, concealing
that it is brief and ambiguous,
the giver of death and life.

And a place only ends
because the man is mortal
in whom the place lived.

AS CASAS

I

As casas vieram de noite
De manhã são casas
À noite estendem os braços para o alto
fumegam vão partir

Fecham os olhos
percorrem grandes distâncias
como nuvens ou navios

As casas fluem de noite
sob a maré dos rios

São altamente mais dóceis
que as crianças
Dentro do estuque se fecham
pensativas

Luiza Neto Jorge

1939–1989. Born in Lisbon. Studied at the University of Lisbon, without taking a degree. Associated with the magazine *Poesia 61,* where she published her second chapbook. Wrote most of her smallish output of poetry in Paris, where she lived from 1962 to 1968. A renowned literary translator, she also worked with several film directors, writings scripts and dialogue.

HOUSES

I
The houses came at night
In the morning they're houses
At night they raise their arms
and release smoke all set to take off

They close their eyes
crossing great distances
like clouds or ships

Houses flow at night
under the rivers' tides

They are far more docile
than children
Closed up inside their plaster
they ponder

Tentam falar bem claro
no silêncio
com sua voz de telhas inclinadas

II

Prometeu ser virgem toda a vida
Desceu persianas sobre os olhos
alimentou-se de aranhas
humidades
raios de sol oblíquos

Quando lhe tocam   quereria fugir
se abriam uma porta
escondia o sexo

Ruiu num espasmo de verão
molhada por um sol masculino

V

Louca como era a da esquina
recebia gente a qualquer hora
Caía em pedaços e
vejam lá convidava as rameiras
os ratos os ninhos de cegonha
apitos de comboio bêbados pianos
como todas as vozes de animais selvagens

IX

O ar
é a casa mais alta
— a mais rica —

desta aldeia

They speak as clearly as they can
in the silence
with their voice of slanting roof tiles

II

She vowed to be a virgin all her life
She lowered the blinds over her eyes
and fed on spiders
dampness
slanting rays of sunlight

When touched   she wanted to flee
if a door was opened
she concealed her sex

She caved in under a summer spasm
all wet from a masculine sun

V

Crazy as the house on the corner was
she took in people at any time of day
She was falling apart and
just think of it invited whores
rats storks' nests train whistles
drunks and pianos
as well as all the voices of wild animals

IX

The air
is the highest
most opulent house

of this village

XII

que não que não queria paredes
que não queria postigos frestas
                    clarabóias

que entrasse ou saísse o mar as marés
dos evadidos
que era só casa
uma s o l i d ã o a b e r t a
não quaisquer quatroparedes infinitas

XIII

Nunca de madeiras tão rijas fosse feita
Sob o meu tecto espancam grávidas
nas câmaras soluçam toda a noite

maldita sou   e me lamento
Os fantasmas circulam   as caveiras
olham-me   sentinelas escarram para o chão
o meu chão de cimento armado

Invoco ao deitar-me um terramoto
um golpe de vento salvador

Em ódio adormeço   em ódio acordo
a alma desfaz-se hora-após-hora
o muro estremece até aos ossos
estreito estreitíssimo alarmado
se afasta   o corredor

Quem me lavará antes da morte?
Quem perfumará meu corpo morto?
A mim casa quem me chorará?

XII

it didn't want didn't want walls
it didn't want little windows, apertures
                skylights

        it wanted the incoming and outgoing sea
the tides of fugitives
it wanted to be just a house
an o p e n s o l i t u d e
not another infinity of four walls

XIII

If only I weren't made of such hard wood
Under my ceiling pregnant women get beaten
they sob all night in the bedrooms

I've been cursed   and I lament my fate
Ghosts roam around   skulls
peer at me   sentries spit on the floor
my floor that's made of reinforced concrete

When I lie down I pray for an earthquake
a blast of liberating wind

I fall asleep revolted   I wake up revolted
my soul crumbles hour by hour
the wall trembles down to my bones
the narrow still narrower hallway
recedes in fear

Who will wash me before I die?
Who will perfume my corpse?
Who will weep for me, the house?

A MAGNÓLIA

A exaltação do mínimo,
e o magnífico relâmpago
do acontecimento mestre
restituem-me a forma
o meu resplendor.

Um diminuto berço me recolhe
onde a palavra se elide
na matéria — na metáfora —
necessária, e leve, a cada um
onde se ecoa e resvala.

A magnólia,
o som que se desenvolve nela
quando pronunciada,
é um exaltado aroma
perdido na tempestade,

um mínimo ente magnífico
desfolhando relâmpagos
sobre mim.

A CASA DO MUNDO

Aquilo que às vezes parece
um sinal no rosto
é a casa do mundo
é um armário poderoso
com tecidos sanguíneos guardados
e a sua tribo de portas sensíveis.

MAGNOLIA

Exaltation of the minimal
and the magnificent lightning
of the master event
restore to me form
my splendour.

A tiny crib cradles me
where the word elides
into matter — metaphor —
as required, almost weightless,
in whom it echoes and slides.

Magnolia,
the sound that swells in it
when pronounced,
is an exalted fragrance
lost in the storm,

a magnificent minimal entity
shedding on me
its lightning leaves.

THE HOUSE OF THE WORLD

Sometimes what seems
to be a birthmark on a face
is the house of the world
is a mighty armoire
with bloody tissues inside
and its tribe of sensitive doors

Cheira a teias eróticas. Arca delirante
arca sobre o cheiro a mar de amar.

Mar fresco. Muros romanos. Toda a música.
O corredor lembra uma corda suspensa entre
os Pirinéus, as janelas entre faces gregas.
Janelas que cheiram ao ar de fora
à núpcia do ar com a casa ardente.

Luzindo cheguei à porta.
Interrompo os objectos de família, atiro-lhes
a porta.
Acendo os interruptores, acendo a interrupção,
as novas paisagens têm cabeça, a luz
é uma pintura clara, mais claramente lembro:
uma porta, um armário, aquela casa.

Um espelho verde de face oval
é que parece uma lata de conservas dilatada
com um tubarão a revirar-se no estômago
no fígado, nos rins, nos tecidos sanguíneos.

É a casa do mundo:
desaparece em seguida.

It smells of erotic cobwebs. A delirious chest
on the scent-of-the-sea of sensuality.

A bracing sea. Roman walls. Any and all music.
The hallway recalls a rope suspended between
the Pyrenees, the windows between Greek faces.
Windows that smell of the air outside,
of the air's marriage to the ardent house.

I reach the door glowing.
I interrupt the family objects, I throw open
the door.
I switch on the lights, switching everything around,
the new landscapes have heads, light
is a clear painting, I remember more clearly:
a door, an armoire, that house.

A green, oval-shaped mirror
seems to be a tin bulging
with a shark writhing in its stomach,
its liver, its kidneys, its bloody tissues.

It's the house of the world:
it's here, it disappears.

LAMENTO POR DIOTIMA

o que vamos fazer amanhã
neste caso de amor desesperado?
ouvir música romântica
ou trepar pelas paredes acima?

amarfanhar-nos numa cadeira
ou ficar fixamente diante
de um copo de vinho ou de uma ravina?
o que vamos fazer amanhã

que não seja um ajuste de contas?
o que vamos fazer amanhã
do que mais se sonhou ou morreu?
numa esquina talvez te atropelem,

Vasco Graça Moura

1942–2014. Born in Oporto. Studied law at the University of Lisbon and worked as a lawyer for a few years. Served as director of Portugal's national publishing house and headed up a number of cultural institutions. Politically outspoken as a centre-right Social Democrat, he held various appointed and elective offices. Prolific as a poet, he was also a novelist, a highly acclaimed translator, and a literary critic noteworthy for his essays on Camões.

LAMENT FOR DIOTIMA

what will we do tomorrow
with so much desperate love?
listen to romantic music
or climb the walls?

crumple ourselves up in a chair
or stupidly linger over
a glass of wine or a ravine?
what will we do tomorrow

that's not a settling of accounts?
what will we do tomorrow
with all we dreamed and all that died?
you might get run over on the street,

num relvado talvez me fuzilem
o teu corpo talvez seja meu,
mas que vamos fazer amanhã
entre as árvores e a solidão?

O MOINHO DE CAFÉ

o moinho de café figura nalguns
quadros dos cubistas, com o jornal, a
garrafa, o cachimbo, tudo em
castanhos e cinzentos. é

a realidade nas suas arestas vivas, a sombria
presença das reduzidas
alucinações: o moinho
de café transformava tudo em fino pó

moído que encravava as engrenagens mais íntimas,
as da paixão e do lamento, ou as caligrafias
lineares de meios perfis e aves azul-cobalto.
mais tarde o moinho de café moeu a representação

que se tornou irreconhecível e deu
lugar a uma música de espirais
menos rotativas, a uma memória
menos angulosa, a uma periferia

menos grata a cézanne, a uma natureza
menos morta, talvez seja isso, a uma
natureza pronta para a desordem
de uma outra virtualidade ou natureza.

o moinho de café tornou-se um realejo.
o mundo acelerou-se,
as vidas ficaram menos lineares
e as águas de cristal ficaram pardas.

i might get shot on a green lawn,
your body might be mine,
but what we will do tomorrow
among the trees and solitude?

THE COFFEE-MILL

the coffee-mill shows up in various
cubist paintings, along with the bottle, the
newspaper and the pipe, all in
browns and greys, reality

with its vital edges, the sombre
presence of reduced
hallucinations. the coffee-mill
turned everything into a finely ground

powder that jammed the most intimate gears,
those of passion and grief, as well as the linear
calligraphies of silhouettes and cobalt-blue birds.
next the coffee-mill ground up representation,

which became unintelligible and gave
way to a music of spirals
less given to spinning, to a memory
less sharply defined, to contours

less indebted to cézanne, to a life
less still — yes, perhaps to a life
that was ready for the disorder
of another kind of life, another nature.

the coffee-mill became a barrel-organ.
the world speeded up,
people's lives became less linear,
and the crystalline waters turned cloudy.

UM CÃO PARA POMPEIA

aos amantes enlaçados contraponho
um cão de pompeia. decerto ele andaria
a brincar junto ao forum, à cata de algum osso,
quando o vesúvio o caçou, mais lesto,

para moldá-lo em pedra-pomes.
insisto em vê-lo como um bicho magro e descuidado,
de penúria diuturna. passou de leve
pelos peristilos, alheio ao luxo, à corrupção,

à astrologia, e nunca dos triclínios
lhe caiu um naco envenenado, nunca se tornou
nem animal simbólico, nem mito que ganisse.
nunca foi encontrado nas escavações, mas é para aqui chamado.

era um cão, just a dog, com pulgas e
que alçava a perna como todos os cães
e ladrava e mordia quando era preciso.
fazia pela vida e, fauno das esquinas, pelas cadelas no cio.

alguma tabuleta diria cave canem em tésseras minúsculas,
sem alaridos da história, e só sobreviveu
nos livros de latim expurgados, misturada
com a guerra das gálias e alguns nomes de deuses.

eu canto um cão sem fábula nem pedigree, que não fugiu aos fados,
um rafeiro vulgar, digamos, de plínio
o velho que, a propósito, morreu perto dali,
talvez uivando, uns dias depois dele.

"você é um cerebral", disse-me cloé, flava e enervada.
"sim", disse-lhe eu com prudência, "mas há tantos.
e o amor e a morte sempre foram pensáveis".
e acrescentei "e depois? que mal faz isso ao cão?"

A DOG FOR POMPEII

rather than a pair of embracing lovers i propose
a dog from pompeii. no doubt he would be
frolicking next to the forum, in search of a bone,
when friskier vesuvius caught and moulded him

into pumice-stone. i insist
on seeing him as a scrawny, neglected creature
for whom poverty was a way of life. he skipped
through peristyles, a stranger to luxury, to corruption,

to astrology, and no poisoned morsel ever befell him
from the triclinia, he never became
a symbolic animal or barking myth.
he was never found in any excavation, but we summon him now.

he was just a dog, un chien, who had fleas and
raised his paw like all dogs
and yelped and bit when necessary. he lived
for his next meal and, faun of street corners, for bitches in heat.

a sign no doubt read *cave canem* in tiny tesserae,
making no mark in history, surviving only
in expurgated latin books, mixed up
with the gallic wars and a few names of gods.

i sing of a dog without fable or pedigree, who didn't escape fate,
an ordinary mutt belonging, let's say, to pliny
the elder, who happens to have died nearby,
perhaps howling, a few days later.

"you're so cerebral," said vexed and golden-haired chloe.
"yes," i replied cautiously, "but so are a lot of other people.
and love and death have always been ponderable."
"besides," i added, "what harm does it do the dog?"

MANEIRAS OITOCENTISTAS

este é o caso flácido da baleia morta
que deu à costa perto da póvoa do varzim:
com o que o bicho sofreu ninguém se importa,
tinha morrido há muito e estava toda torta.
em todo o caso bem dava um folhetim.

teria sido baleia forasteira.
é fácil de supô-la todo o verão
a dar às barbatanas, hercúlea, galhofeira,
o seu ledo repuxo tomava sempre a dianteira.
podre gerava agora só focos de infecção.

toneladas de banha, imensas, imprevistas,
vinham sabe-se lá de que ignotas águas fundas,
sem jonas na barriga, mas provocando imundas,
repentinas tonturas nos banhistas.

FANNY

fanny, a grande
amiga de minha mãe,
ossuda, esgalgada,
de cabelo escuro e curto,
e filha de uma inglesa,

tinha um sentido prático
extraordinário e era
muito emancipada, para
os costumes da foz
daquele tempo.

IN THE MANNER OF THE NINETEENTH CENTURY

this is the flaccid case of a dead whale
that beached on portugal's northern coast.
no one cared about the creature's travails:
it was long dead, its corpse beyond the pale,
but it was still good for an anecdote.

it must have been a foreign-born whale
that, during the summer, lost its direction,
forever flexing its flippers and playing,
its happy spout continually spraying.
now it did nothing but breed infection.

those tons of enormously blubbery layers
came from who knows what watery depths,
with no jonah in the belly but causing dreadful
bouts of dizziness in the bathers.

FANNY

fanny, lanky and with
short dark hair,
english on her
mother's side and
my mother's best friend,

was extraordinarily
practical and very
emancipated
for those days
in oporto society.

uma vez, estando
sozinha no cinema, sentiu
a mão do homem a
seu lado deslizar-lhe
pela coxa. prestou-se a isso e

deixou-a estar assim,
com toda a placidez. mas abriu
discretamente a carteira de pelica,
tirou a tesourinha das unhas
e quando a mão no escuro

se imobilizou mais tépida,
apunhalou-a num gesto
seco, enérgico, cirúrgico.
o homem deu um salto
por sobre os assentos e

fugiu num súbito
relincho da
mão furada.
fanny foi sempre
de um grande despacho,

na sua solidão muito
ocupada num escritório. um dia
atirou-se da janela
do quinto andar
e pronto.

once, when on her own
at the cinema, she felt
the hand of the man
next to her sliding over
her thigh. she let it slide

without flinching, perfectly
calm, while discreetly
opening her leather purse
to remove her nail scissors,
and when the hand in the dark

rested, growing warmer,
she stabbed it with a quick,
forceful, surgical stroke.
the man jumped up
in his seat and

fled screaming
with his punctured
hand. fanny
was always a model
of efficiency,

in her busy solitude
at an office job. one day
she jumped out the fifth
floor window and that
was that.

PRIMEIRAS MORADAS

8

o que sinto, esta tarde, não ficou
torcido nas palavras,
no terraço florido onde procuras
alguma direcção, indícios,
esse teu sentimento, ardil doirado.
a viração

mudou o chão da hora, a cor do dia.
levanto-me
com as tuas palavras acordadas,
como são boas as tuas tendas,
as tuas moradas,
como ribeiros se estendem,

António Franco Alexandre

Born 1944, in Viseu, north-central Portugal. Studied Mathematics in Toulouse (1962–69) and at Harvard University (1969–71), and Philosophy in Paris (1971–74). Earned his PhD in Philosophy at the University of Lisbon, where he has taught this subject since 1975. Published his first book of poems, *Distância,* in 1969, but excluded it from his collected poetry.

DWELLING PLACES – I

8

what I feel today didn't get
twisted in words
on the flowering terrace where you seek
direction, clues, your own
feeling, that golden snare.
the wind

shifted the day's colour, the ground
of this moment. I rouse
to your wide-awake words:
how good are your tents,
your dwellings.
like far stretching streams,

como jardins ao pé do rio, sua semente
estará em muitas águas.
assim acertes em palavras não
mas no jeito que têm nas esquinas,
e contra mim eleves o seu muro,
tuas tendas, Jacob, tuas moradas.

11

Sobre poemas de Avraham ben Ytzhak

por sete caminhos, uma lua, um veneno,
por sete caminhos partimos,
na mochila do ar, no barco do vento.
na floresta azul logo nos perdemos,
na estrada, no medo, no mudo segredo,
pelas sete partidas nos rompemos.

ao dia o dia um sol cinzento lega
a noite a outra noite se lamenta
amanhã morreremos sem palavras.
e no dia da marcha estaremos à porta
e próximos enfim, se o coração exulta.

o dia ao dia dá um sol, radiante,
a noite em outra noite verte estrelas,
felizes que semeiam e não colhem,
sabem que o seu coração está clamando no deserto
nos seus lábios floresce o silêncio.
por sete caminhos partimos, por um regressamos.

like gardens by the river, their seed
will be in many waters.
don't choose words for themselves
but for how they stand at corners
and against me raise their wall,
your tents, Jacob, your dwellings.

11

On poems by Avraham ben Ytzhak

by seven paths, a moon, a poison,
by seven paths we depart,
in the air's knapsack, in the wind's boat.
we soon get lost in the blue woods,
on the road, in fear, in the untold secret,
unto the ends of the earth we break our bodies.

the day bequeaths a grey sun to the day,
one night complains to another,
tomorrow we'll die without words.
and on the day of the march we'll be at the door,
together at last, if the heart rejoice.

the day gives a radiant sun to the day,
the night pours stars into another night,
happy those who sow and don't reap:
they know their heart is crying in the desert,
silence flowers on their lips.
by seven paths we depart, by one we return.

SEGUNDAS MORADAS

15

quando ele criou o céu e a terra, e os deuses,
pôs este monte diante de mim,
assim completo,
mas eu não tinha corpo: era, talvez, um sopro
menos aéreo, no ar.
e não havia luz, mas só no escuro
o Manto cintilava.
isto sabes que sei. o resto

é a razão de ser desta viagem, a diligência
encharcada de senso e de chuvisco,
a noite, na estalagem, o fantasma,
o imenso cenário que desaba...
se é tudo tão perfeito no palácio,
a mesa posta, e o rápido cometa
capaz de transportar além de nada,
que vitória, de asas douradas tão exactamente no mármore,

celebrará as nossas vidas?
espero uma resposta antes do fim das
principais lavouras,
a colheita desigual, tórridas tempestades
varrendo de lado a lado o continente,
pragas de sapos, gafanhotos, pulgas,
o medo a afiar facas na cozinha,
antes do sangue.

DWELLING PLACES – II

15

when he created heaven and earth, and the gods,
he placed before me this mound,
complete and whole.
but I had no body: perhaps I was a less airy
breath in the air.
and there was no light, only the Mantle
shimmering in the dark.
this much you know I know. the rest

is the reason for this journey, the coach
drenched with meaning and drizzle,
night-time, at the inn, the ghost,
the vast stage set that collapses...
if the palace is in perfect order,
the table all set, and the swift comet
can transport us beyond nothingness,
what victory with exquisitely gilded marble wings

will celebrate our lives?
I hope for an answer before the end of
ploughing and planting,
the unequal harvest, torrid storms
raging across the continent,
plagues of toads, locusts, fleas,
fear whetting its knives in the kitchen,
before the blood.

18

e no detalhe
habita um deus: partilho
essa convicção simples, dura como um seixo.
de todas as palavras, só uma irá bater
à porta do desconhecido,
entrar no coração, dar as boas-vindas,
e todas poderão ruir, e ela ficará latejando
no sangue de primeiras núpcias.

eu calculo a passagem do estorninho e da poupa, vejo
a exacta emoção da inexacta curva,
o rastro, facilmente luminoso.
a terra cresce para todos nós, tão rápida nos ramos,
só o vento a detém. um dia
seremos úteis e preciosos como a erva e a cabra,
e ricos de virtudes saberemos
o que fazer para morrer, não morrer. entretanto

ela lateja na núpcia do sangue, inteiramente ignorante
do grande sentido de tudo isto,
egoísta como a primeira mão
que nos tocou,
um destino leviano, sensível, pacato,
depois o sulco deixado reparte as colinas
e o pequeno piano repete
a criação do mundo.

20

as primeiras coisas eram verdes ou azuis, com água pela cintura;
duras esmeraldas umas, outras animais, vibrantes
quando lhes toca a luz; o mais das vezes encostados

18

and in each detail
a god lives: I share
this conviction, simple and hard as a pebble.
of all the words that exist, just one will knock
at the stranger's door,
enter into the heart, offer warm welcome,
and though all the rest crumble, it will still throb
in the blood of that first marriage.

I calculate the flight of the hoopoe and starling, I note
the exact emotion of the inexact curve,
the trail that easily glows.
swiftly in the branches the earth grows for us all,
hindered only by the wind. one day
we'll be useful and precious like grass and goats,
and, rich in virtues, we'll know what we need to do
to die, not die. meanwhile

the word throbs in the blood's marriage, blind
to the larger meaning of all this,
selfish like the first hand
that touched us,
a casual, cosy, sensible destiny,
and the furrow left behind divides the hills
and the little piano repeats
the creation of the world.

20

the first things were green or blue and waist-high in water:
hard emeralds, for instance, or animals that shiver
when touched by the light, their bodies pressing

à parede do estábulo, com grandes olhos húmidos
e um precipício ao fundo (e as nuvens são o seu bafo).
e no entanto, visto à distância exacta, tudo se transforma:
o cenário do mundo é só um infinito espaço
cheio de coisa nenhuma, e a luz o puro efeito
de dois deuses menores que marcam o compasso.

é certo que, na chuva, o teu corpo anuncia
com seu distante olhar, um prazer que não cabe
na estreiteza da fábula; um céu, não duvidemos,
acolhe o terno gesto que não foi.
já na parede a meio branca traço, a contragosto,
o tempo mal passado que apodrece; e ruminante encosto
ao tampo de água o bico ou pincel fosco
onde surgira, de repente, nada.

os portões oscilam, e a erva adiante, se nos aproximamos.
claramente vejo como te divides
num infinito número simultâneo de mundos.
as palavras celebram, mudas, a água na paisagem,
verde ou azul, conforme desejaste.
avanço imóvel, descalço sobre a erva,
e quando fecho os olhos invade-me a luz por dentro
compacta, completa, como as coisas primeiras.

22

meio da tarde em campo de besteiros: água, pequena e fria,
caindo do granito; e na penumbra,
as flechas. penso: não poderei jamais
esquecer este sítio, este limite,
a serena harmonia de colinas e corpos.

against the stable wall, with large wet eyes and an abyss
in the depths (and the clouds are their breath)
but when viewed from the right distance, everything changes:
the world's stage is just an endless space
full of nothing, and light merely the effect
of two minor gods keeping time.

it's true that, in the rain, your body announces
with its faraway gaze a pleasure that doesn't fit
in the bounds of the fable: a sky, to be sure,
receives the tender gesture not made.
I reluctantly draw on the dull white wall
time poorly spent and now rotting; ruminating, I press
to the shield of water the blunt beak or brush
where suddenly nothing emerged.

the gate swings, and the grass beyond it, if we draw near.
I clearly see how you divide
into an infinite number of simultaneous worlds.
voiceless words celebrate water in the landscape,
green or blue, however you wanted it.
barefoot I advance, without moving, over the grass,
and when I close my eyes I'm filled with a light
that's compact, complete, like the first things.

22

mid-afternoon in campo de besteiros*: tiny, icy water
falling from the granite, and in the shade
the arrows. I think: I'll never be able
to forget this place, this boundary,
the tranquil harmony of hills and bodies.

* Campo de Besteiros, whose name means "crossbowmen's field", is a village near the town of Viseu, in north-central Portugal.

mas tu escondes a boca com as mãos, e já a noite
anónima nos funde; a nuvem cobre campos desolados,
e a paciente traça rói o arco-íris.

vou ficando invisível, aos pedaços,
comendo laranjas no escuro.
o teu corpo é dos que nunca lêem livros,
sabem de estradas e de pássaros, pouco mais;
a tua morada tem no telhado as frinchas
da lei, onde se vê o céu; e eu,
absorto de silêncio e de chuvisco,
ó tosco cantador!,

dissolvo-me na sombra da paisagem,
separo-me de nós, de mim, serei só quase
a chama no carvão que fica ardendo
noite fora. noite fora.
acordaremos, já sei, transparentes e sábios,
do outro lado da criação do mundo;
uma mão presa à luz, outra nas trevas,
um só tronco de chamas, uma asa.

but your hands hide your mouth, and already we're merging
in the anonymous night; clouds cover desolate fields,
and the patient moth gnaws the rainbow.

limb by limb I turn invisible,
eating oranges in the dark.
yours is one of those bodies that never read books,
that know roads and birds, little else;
your dwelling's roof has the chinks prescribed
by custom, allowing us to see the sky, and I,
a clumsy songster! absorbed
by silence and drizzle,

dissolve in the landscape's shadows,
withdrawing from us, from me, to become almost
just the flame in the embers burning
far into the night. into the night.
we will awaken, I know, wise and transparent,
on the other side of the world's creation,
one hand touching light, the other wrapped in darkness,
one blazing log, a single wing.

SALSUGEM

2

queria ser marinheiro correr mundo
com as mãos abertas ao rumo das aves costeiras
a boca magoando-se na visão das viagens
levaria na bagagem a sonolenta canção dos ventos
e a infindável espera do país assustado pelas águas

debruçou-se para o outro lado do espelho
onde o corpo se torna aéreo até aos ossos
a noite devolveu-lhe outro corpo vogando
ao abandono dum secreto regresso... depois
guardou a paixão de longínquos dias no saco de lona
e do fundo nostálgico do espelho
surgiram os súbitos olhos do mar

Al Berto

1948–1997. Pseudonym of Alberto R. Pidwell Tavares. Born in Coimbra but raised on grandfather's farm in Sines, a town on Portugal's southwestern coast. Attended art school in Lisbon as an adolescent, and in 1967 — to avoid being drafted to fight in Africa — he moved to Belgium, where he studied painting for several years. His interest shifted to literature, and he collaborated in fringe publications, writing in French. While based in Brussels, he travelled to France, Spain, Italy and Greece. Returned to Portugal in 1975. Opened a bookshop and small publishing house in Sines. Moved to Lisbon in 1987.

SALT SPRAY

2

he wanted to be a sailor and tour the world
to open his hands to the paths of coastal birds
to feel his mouth hurt from the vision of voyages
in his baggage he'd take the hypnotic song of winds
and the endless waiting of that country scared of the waters

he leaned into the other side of the mirror
where the body becomes airy down to its bones
the night restored to him the other body drifting
in the wake of a secret return... then he stowed
in his duffel bag the passion of distant days
and the sudden eyes of the ocean stared at him
from the nostalgic depths of the mirror

cresceram-lhe búzios nas pálpebras algas finas
moviam-se medusas luminosas ao alcance da fala
e o peito era o extenso areal
onde as lendas e as crónicas tinham esquecido
enigmáticos esqueletos insectos e preciosos metais

um fio de sémen atava o coração devassado pela salsugem
o corpo separava-se da milenar sombra
imobilizava-se no sono antigo da terra
descia ao esquecimento de tudo... navegava
no rumor das águas oxidadas agarrava-se à raiz das espadas
ia de mastro em mastro perscrutando a insónia
abrindo ácidos lumes pelo rosto incerto dalgum mar

3

era um barco
onde os homens regressavam como um lamento
tinham saudades de ilhas... embebedavam-se
no receio de nunca chegar
deitados nas tábuas de sarro do porão
com o cio da noite pegando-se aos membros húmidos
esperavam que se avistasse terra
onde pudessem enfim reabastecer-se de alimentos
água fresca... e quem sabe se uma carta não bastava
para saciar as sedes e as fomes do irrequieto coração

assim se quedavam paralisados
os ventres roçando as cordas... as vagas contra o casco
suspirando mansos olhavam depois
a baba acetinada dos peixes voando

era um barco
uma sombra do mar com o sol tatuado à proa... avançava
como avançam as vozes aquáticas pelos sonhos adentro

seashells grew on his silken seaweed eyelids
glowing jellyfish twitched within reach of his speech
and his chest was the sandy expanse
where legends and the chronicles had left behind
enigmatic skeletons insects precious metals

a thread of semen girded his salt-wracked heart
his body broke away from the millenary shadow
hovered statically in the earth's ancient sleep
and descended into the universal oblivion... he sailed
in the swish of rusty waters clutching the root of swords
going from mast to mast probing his insomnia
opening acid fires in the hazy visage of some sea

3

it was a ship
whose men were returning like a long lament
pining after islands... they got drunk
out of fear they'd never arrive
they lay flat on the slimy boards of the hold
with the lust of night clinging to their humid members
they hoped to sight land
so as to finally restock with food
fresh water... and perhaps a letter would be enough
to slake the thirst and hunger of their restive hearts

they lay there as if paralyzed
their bellies grazing the ropes as waves lapped the hull
they sighed softly then gazed
at the glossy drool of the flying fish

it was a ship
a seaborne shadow with the sun tattooed on its prow... it moved
forward
the way aquatic voices move through dreams

perturbando a navegação da memória
era um barco
com o velame cansado e as mãos calejadas
pelas tempestades das sete partidas do mundo

chegava ao porto
descarregava palavras dialectos estilhaços de concha
espinhas pedaços de corda que na incerteza dos dias
alinhava pelo cais vislumbrado doutro corpo
e voltava a partir
evitando o silencioso plâncton dos espelhos
acostando somente à memória dalgum distante lugar
onde o amor largou sobre o corpo-amante
uma esteira de conhecidas e sangrentas mercadorias

4

às vezes... quando acordava
era porque tínhamos chegado

ficava a bordo encostado às amuradas
horas a fio
espiava a cidade e as colinas inclinando-se
para a noite lodosa do rio
e o balouçar do barco enchia-me de melancolia

a noite trazia-me aragens com cheiro a corpos suados
cantares e danças em redor de fogos que eu não sabia
o ruído dos becos a luz fosca dum bar
se descesse a terra encontrar-te-ia... tinha a certeza
para o voo frenético do sexo
e num suspiro talvez alargássemos os umbrais da noite
mas ficava preso ao navio... hipnotizado
com o coração em desordem
os dedos explorando nervosos as ranhuras da madeira
os pregos ferrugentos as cordas

disturbing the navigation of memory
it was a ship
with its rigging exhausted and its hands calloused
from the storms of the four corners of the world

it sailed into port
to unload words dialects shards of seashells
fish bones and lengths of rope that in the days' uncertainty
were tied against the dock descried in another body
and it departed again
avoiding the silent plankton of mirrors
nearing only the coast of some remotely remembered place
where love had left on the lover-body
a cargo of familiar and bloody goods

4

sometimes... when i woke up
it was because we'd arrived

i'd stay on board leaning against the rails of the deck
for hours on end
observing the city the hills bowing
toward the river's muddy night
and the ship's gentle rocking filled me with melancholy

the night brought me breezes with smells of sweaty bodies
songs and dances around unfamiliar fires
the racket of alleyways the dim light of a bar
if i went ashore i was sure to find you
for the frenetic flight of sex
and with a sigh we might flood the threshold of night
but i remained shipbound... mesmerized
with my heart in a jumble
my nervous fingers exploring the cracks in the wood
the rusty nails the ropes

as luzes do cais revelavam-me corpos fugidios
penumbras donde se escapavam ditos obscenos
gemidos agudos sibilantes risos que despertavam em mim
a vontade sempre urgente de partir

the lights on the wharf disclosed fleeing bodies
shadows enveloping obscene remarks
sharp moans shrill laughs that aroused in me
the forever urgent desire to depart

BALDIO

No campo, os rebanhos confundem-se com o verde
das pastagens, como se fosse a erva a comê-los;
e o balido das cabras e o som dos guizos, que
se misturam com o latido dos cães, escondem
também eles a voz do pastor, que nada diz acerca
do destino (supondo que um rebanho tem destino).

No campo, ninguém vê para onde vão esses rebanhos
quando, à tarde, atravessam a estrada e obrigam
os carros a parar. Por vezes, um condutor insiste
em abrir caminho através das peles e dos chifres; mas
os cães metem-se à frente do carro, como se ele
fizesse parte do rebanho, e forçam-no a desviar-se.

Há regras a seguir neste mundo, que a natureza
humana não consegue alterar. É como se campo

Nuno Júdice

Born in 1949, in Mexilhoeira Grande, the Algarve. Did his high school and university studies in Lisbon, receiving his PhD in Romance Languages and Literature at the Universidade Nova [New University], where he is a full professor. Lived in Bern in the 1980s and from 1997 to 2004 in Paris, where he was cultural attaché to the Portuguese Embassy. An active participant in and promoter of cultural events, he has served as the editor of several Portuguese literary reviews.

PASTURE

In the country, grazing herds merge with
the green, as if the grass were eating them,
and the goats' bleating and bells' ringing, which
blend with the dogs' barking, also hide the voice
of the goatherd, who says nothing about their
destination (assuming a herd has a destination).

In the country, no one sees where these herds are
going when, at dusk, they cross the road and force
the cars to stop. Sometimes a motorist attempts
to cut through the hides and horns, but
the dogs face the car head-on, as if it
were part of the herd, and make it veer away.

The world has its rules that human nature cannot
change. It's as if the country and animals

e animais formassem um só corpo; como se
nenhum de nós conseguisse entrar nesse
obscuro mundo de leis e direções invisíveis. E até
o pastor, em silêncio, parece guiado pelos deuses.

DEUS

À noite, há um ponto do corredor
em que um brilho ocasional faz lembrar
um pirilampo. Inclino-me para o apanhar
— e a sombra apaga-o. Então,
levanto-me: já sem a preocupação
de saber o que é esse brilho, ou
do que é reflexo.
Ali, no entanto, ficou
uma inquietação; e muito tempo depois,
sem me dar conta do motivo autêntico,
ainda me volto no corredor, procurando a luz

MELANCOLIA

O rosto que se perde entre os outros rostos
não é o dele. É o de quem não sabe quem é; o
de uma sombra que fica por detrás da luz. A
diferença de um rosto para outro, por vezes,
não é nada; e só o que sobra de um olhar, cuja
circunstância se esqueceu, pode fazer com
que os olhos se lembrem de outros olhos, ou
uma cor súbita, na tarde de chuva, levante
as nuvens do espírito, o inverno da alma,
e traga o movimento em falso de uma luz de

formed a single body, as if none of us could
penetrate that obscure realm of invisible
laws and directions. And even the goatherd
seems, in silence, to be guided by the gods.

GOD

At night there's a point in the hallway
where an occasional glimmer suggests
a firefly. I bend down to grab it
— and the darkness swallows it. And so
I straighten up, no longer concerned
to know what that glimmer is or
what it reflects.
But an uneasiness
remains, and much later, without grasping
the real motive, I turn around
in the hallway, seeking the light
that no longer exists.

MELANCHOLY

The face lost among other faces isn't his.
It's the face of a man who doesn't know who he is,
the face of a shadow forever behind the light.
The difference between two faces is sometimes
nothing; and only what survives from a gaze whose
circumstance we've forgotten can make our eyes
recall other eyes, or cause a sudden colour
on a rainy afternoon to lift clouds
from the mind, winter from the soul,
evoking the false note of a spring

primavera, tão breve como as palavras que
dizem o amor, e como o amor tão breve.

POESIA

De onde vem — a voz que
nos rasgou por dentro, que
trouxe consigo a chuva negra
do outono, que fugiu por
entre névoas e campos
devorados pela erva?

Esteve aqui — aqui dentro
de nós, como se sempre aqui
tivesse estado; e não a
ouvimos, como se não nos
falasse desde sempre,
aqui, dentro de nós.

E agora que a queremos ouvir,
como se a tivéssemos re-
conhecido outrora, onde está? A voz
que dança de noite, no inverno,
sem luz nem eco, enquanto
segura pela mão o fio
obscuro do horizonte.

Diz: "Não chores o que te espera,
nem desças já pela margem
do rio derradeiro. Respira,
numa breve inspiração, o cheiro
da resina, nos bosques, e
o sopro húmido dos versos."

Como se a ouvíssemos.

glow, as brief as the words that tell
love, and as brief as the love told.

POETRY

Where is it from — the voice
that tore us up inside,
brought us autumn's
black rain, and fled
through fogs and fields
overrun by wild grass?

It was here, inside of us,
as if it had always been
inside of us. And we didn't
hear it, as if it hadn't
always been talking to us
here, inside of us.

And now that we want to hear
it, as if we used to know it,
where is it? The voice
that dances at night, in winter,
without light or echo,
while taking in its hand
the horizon's shadowy thread...

It says: "Don't weep over what
will come. Don't go down yet
to the final river. Breathe,
in a short breath, the smell
of the woods' resin and
the light dew of verses."

As if we had heard it.

ALEGORIA (explicação)

Nas noites de inverno, com a chuva a cair,
olhai a mendiga: procurando, no chão,
entre papéis velhos, o retrato da rainha que foi;
e rezando, entre dentes, a ladainha que ouviu
ao príncipe que a deixou.

Com as mãos, arruma as folhas como lenços
preciosos. Molhadas, a luz fá-las transparentes:
sedas de um reino sem pés descalços, nem
corpos ao frio, nem sequer esse olhar que
implora o sonho da morte.

De manhã, dão com ela deitada: flor
usada, sobre as pedras da calçada.

ÚLTIMA CEIA

Com que monotonia penso em mim;
sentimento distante, que me põem à frente,
na mesa, já frio e sem gosto. Mas vou
comendo, sem pressa, este prato
indigesto; e, a cada garfada, antecipo
a dor de estômago que me irá encher
de pesadelos a noite. Eu: pesada
refeição que não desejo,
mas me puseram à frente.

(E se disser que não como?)

ALLEGORY (explanation)

On winter nights, with the rain falling,
see the beggar searching the littered street
for a picture of the queen she once was
and muttering, between her teeth, the drivel
she heard from the prince who left her.

Her hands arrange the paper scraps like precious
scarves. Wet, they become transparent in the light:
silks of a kingdom without bare feet or shivering
bodies or those eyes that implore
the dream of death.

In the morning they find her lying there:
a discarded flower on the paving stones.

LAST SUPPER

How monotonous to think about me:
a distant sensation heaped
on my plate, already cold and tasteless.
But slowly I eat this indigestible
dish, imagining, with each forkful,
the stomach ache that will fill
my sleep with nightmares. I: a heavy
meal I do not want
but find on my plate.

(And if I refuse to eat it?)

DECADÊNCIA

Quando Roma caiu sob o ataque dos Bárbaros,
os limites do Império ainda se mantiveram. De facto,
a notícia demorou semanas a chegar; e tanto
escravos como senhores pensaram que o Imperador
mantinha o seu poder, que o mundo não vacilava
nos seus eixos, e que o sol que vinha do Oriente
nada vira de novo no seu curso. "Para quê manter
os gestos inalteráveis do passado?", perguntaram,
quando o mensageiro de veste esfarrapada gritou
a notícia terrível. As mulheres calaram-se; excepto
aquela que chorou até ao cair da noite, e depois
partiu para não se voltar a saber dela. Os homens
olharam para o mar, como se ali estivesse uma solução.

Quando um mundo acaba, não é só o vazio que
enche os corações com o seu peso de dúvida;
também as palavras se desfazem no espírito
que interroga o passado. E para todos os lados
onde se olhe, o horizonte parece fechar-se;
só a terra, que espera ainda as primeiras chuvas
do outono, oferece como resposta um seco silêncio,
a imagem de raízes quebradas pelo estio, e
um repouso de covas abertas pelos animais
em busca de refúgio para o assédio da noite.

DECADENCE

When Rome fell to the Barbarians, the outskirts
of the Empire were still intact. In fact it took
weeks for the news to arrive, slaves as well as
masters being convinced that the Emperor
still reigned, that the world's axes were not
swerving, and that the sun coming from the East
had seen nothing new in its journey. "Why keep
using the same old rituals?" they asked
when the messenger with torn clothes shouted
the terrible news. The women kept quiet, except
for the one who wept until nightfall and then
departed, never to be heard of again. The men
gazed at the sea, as if it held a solution.

When a world ends, it's not just that emptiness
fills hearts with its weight of uncertainty;
there's also a crumbling of words in the mind
that questions the past. And whichever way
one looks, the horizon seems to be closing.
Only the earth, still waiting for the first rains
of autumn, offers as a response its arid silence,
the image of roots broken by summer, and
the repose of holes dug by animals
seeking shelter before the siege of night.

A VERDADE HISTÓRICA

A minha filha partiu uma tigela
na cozinha.
E eu que me apetecia escrever
sobre o evento,
tive que pôr de lado inspiração e lápis,
pegar numa vassoura e varrer
a cozinha.

A cozinha varrida de tigela
ficou diferente da cozinha
de tigela intacta:
local propício a escavação e estudo,
curto mapa arqueológico
num futuro remoto.

Uma tigela de louça branca
com flores,

Ana Luísa Amaral

Born in 1956, in Lisbon. Moved with her family at the age of nine to a small town just north of Oporto. Spent two years at Brown University as a Visiting Researcher (1991-93). Earned a PhD in North American Literature with a thesis on Emily Dickinson at the University of Oporto (1995), where she spent many years teaching American and English Literature, Comparative Poetics, Gender Studies and Queer Studies. Retired in 2014 but still pursues her research interests.

HISTORICAL TRUTH

My daughter broke a bowl
in the kitchen.
And I, who felt like writing
about the event,
had to put inspiration and pencil aside,
grab a broom, and sweep
the kitchen.

The kitchen swept of bowl
was different from the kitchen
of the bowl still whole:
a promising site for excavation and study,
a terse archaeological map
in some distant future.

A white porcelain bowl stamped
with flowers,

restos de cereais tratados
em embalagem estanque
espalhados pelo chão.

Não eram grãos de trigo de Pompeia,
mas eram respeitosos cereais
de qualquer forma.
E a tigela, mesmo não sendo da dinastia Ming,
mas das Caldas,
daqui a cinco ou dez mil anos
devia ter estatuto admirativo.

Mas a hecatombe
deu-se.
E escorregada de pequeninas mãos,
ficou esquecida de famas e proveitos,
varrida de vassouras e memórias.

Por mísero e cruel balde de lixo
azul
em plástico moderno
(indestrutível)

COISAS DE PARTIR

Tento empurrar-te de cima do poema
para não o estragar na emoção de ti:
olhos semi-cerrados, em precauções de tempo
a sonhá-lo de longe, todo livre sem ti.

Dele ausento os teus olhos, sorriso, boca, olhar:
tudo coisas de ti, mas coisas de partir...
E o meu alarme nasce: e se morreste aí,
no meio de chão sem texto que é ausente de ti?

and remnants of processed
vacuum-packed cereal
scattered on the floor.

Though not grains of wheat from Pompeii,
they were still respectable
flakes of cereal.
And the bowl, despite being from Caldas
rather than Ming Dynasty,
would have attained an admirable status
in five or ten thousand years.

Then came the hecatomb.
Slipping out of tiny hands,
it was forgotten
by fame and usefulness,
swept by brooms and from memories.

Into the cruel and humiliating blue
trash bin
crafted from modern, indestructible
plastic

ALL SO FRAGILE

I try to push you from off the poem
lest I ruin it with the emotion you stir:
eyes half-closed, guarding against time,
I dream of it from afar, free without you.

I purge from it your eyes, smile, lips, gaze:
things that are you but all so fragile...
And panic strikes: what if you die there
on the floor with no text, fatally expurgated?

E se já não respiras? Se eu não te vejo mais
por te querer empurrar, lírica de emoção?
E o meu pânico cresce: se tu não estiveres lá?
E se tu não estiveres onde o poema está?

Faço eroticamente respiração contigo:
primeiro um advérbio, depois um adjectivo,
depois um verso todo em emoção e juras.
E termino contigo em cima do poema,
presente indicativo, artigos às escuras.

IREI AGORA CARREGAR O TEMPO

Irei agora carregar o tempo
de mil relâmpagos,
tempestades de agosto
e algum rio.
E nele falarei sem
sequer trovas

Habitarei as coisas de tal forma
como a lareira esguia do meu lado,
o tempo carregado de chamas
e de mim

Do tecto desta sala pendem coisas
muito antigas de usar,
mas o que mais me atrai é a chaleira:
tão de ferro e polida,
terá mais de cem anos e uma história
com águas e com tempo,
antes deste seu tecto
— e a solidão

And if you quit breathing? If I see you no more
for pushing you away, lyrical with emotion?
My panic grows: and if you're not there?
What if you're not there where the poem is?

Erotically I breathe in and out with you:
first an adverb, then an adjective, then
a verse that's pure emotion and declarations.
And I end up with you on top of the poem,
in the simple present, articles in the dark.

I'M GOING TO LOAD TIME

I'm going to load time
with a thousand bolts
of lightning, August storms
and some river.
In it I'll speak without
even using verses

I'll inhabit things in the way
of this fireplace, its slender chimney,
time loaded with flames
and with me

From the ceiling in this room hang
things used long ago,
but what most attracts me is the teapot:
so iron, so polished, perhaps a hundred
years old, it has a history
in waters and time,
from before its current ceiling
and solitude

Recorda-me a paixão ainda verde,
as chamas do inferno a consumi-la
sem nunca a destruir.
E uma noite de vento e tempestade,
com que uma vez me assassinei de amor,
e incendiei dezembro

PALIMPSESTO

Limpa o cesto bem limpo,
mas deixa lá ficar sombra ligeira:
essa primeira sílaba.
Sobre ela
podes encher o cesto com mais sílabas,
e até outras palavras.

Terás assim um cesto
que aos olhos de quem vê
é um cesto só teu,
onde escondeste as coisas
do costume dos cestos: flores, solidões,
rastilhos, bombas.

Foi limpo o cesto
aos olhos de quem vê,
mas tu sabes que não.
Que houve ali um momento de ladrão,
quando nele ficou
a sombra dessa sílaba.

E agora mostras
a toda a gente o cesto,
e não há sombra.
Há só a mão que surge
e pega no teu cesto,
o toma devagar.

It reminds me of passion still young,
consumed by hell's flames
yet never destroyed.
And of a night with wind and storms
where once I killed myself with love
and set December on fire

PALIMPSEST

Empty everything out of the basket,
but leave behind a shadow:
that first syllable.
To it you can add
more syllables and even words,
until you fill the basket.

And so you'll have a basket
that to outside eyes
is only your basket,
where you've hidden the things
that baskets hide: flowers, solitudes,
fuses, bombs.

To outside eyes
the basket was completely emptied,
but you know otherwise:
that there was a moment of pilfery,
when that shadow of a syllable
was allowed to stay.

And now you show
the basket to everyone
and there's no shadow.
There's just a hand that appears
and grasps your basket
and slowly takes it,

E o olha com olhos de quem lê,
e o limpa muito limpo,
ao teu antigo cesto,
deixando lá no fundo,
disfarçada,
uma segunda sílaba.

A VITÓRIA DE SAMOTRÁCIA

Se eu deixasse de escrever poemas em
tom condicional, e o tom de conclusão
passasse a solução mais que perfeita,
seria quase igual a Samotrácia.

Cabeça ausente, mas curva bem lançada
do corpo da prosódia em direcção ao sul,
mediterrânica, jubilosa, ardente, leopardo
musical e geometria contaminada
por algum navio. A linha de horizonte:

qualquer linha, por onde os astros morressem
e nascessem, outra feita de fio de fino aço,
e outra ainda onde o teu rosto me contemplasse
ao longe, e me sorrisse sem condição que fosse.

Ter várias formas as linhas do amor: não viver
só de mar ou de planície, nem embalada
em fogo. Que diriam então ou que dirias?

O corpo da prosódia transformado em
corpo de verdade, as pregas do poema,
agora pregas de um vestido longo, tapando
levemente joelho e tornozelo. E não de pedra,
nunca já de pedra. Mas de carne e com
asas —

then looks at it, as if reading,
and then empties everything out
of what used to be your basket,
leaving at the bottom,
well disguised,
a second syllable.

THE VICTORY OF SAMOTHRACE

If I stopped writing poems in a conditional
tone, and adopted the tone of conclusion
as the present perfect solution,
it would be almost equal to Samothrace:

head missing, but the curve of its prosodic
body lunging ardently, jubilantly,
Mediterraneanly southward, a musical
leopard, its geometry fatally marked
by some ship. The horizon:

an abstract line where stars die and are
born, another line made of fine steel wire,
and yet another where your face observes me
from afar, smiling without any conditions.

The lines of love taking various forms: me
not living only off sea or plains, nor bundled
in fire. What would they, or you, say then?

The prosodic body turned into a real
body, the folds of the poem now folds
of a flowing dress that lightly covers
knee and ankle. And not made of stone,
no more stone. But of flesh and with
wings —

DOIS CIPRESTES

O que foi atado
na Terra
continua atado
no Céu
e o que foi desatado
na Terra
continua desatado
no Céu
(no Inferno
é ao contrário)
mas o que não chegou
a ser atado na Terra?
penso em ti
meu marido
não vivemos
no mesmo século

Adília Lopes

Pseudonym of Maria José de Oliveira, **born in 1960,** in Lisbon. Studied Physics at the University of Lisbon but quit before earning a degree, due to a schizoaffective disorder. At that point she began writing, and switched her course of study to Linguistics and Literature (1983–1988). Has done some work in literary archives.

TWO CYPRESSES

What was bound
on Earth
will be bound
in Heaven
and what was loosed
on Earth
will be loosed
in Heaven
(in Hell it's the other
way around)
but what about what never
got bound on Earth?
I think about you
my husband
we didn't live
in the same century

nem na mesma cidade
nunca nos cruzámos
porque não pudemos
procurámo-nos
um ao outro
lavados em lágrimas
a ver os outros
namorarem-se
às três pancadas
eu li o *Yoga para grávidas*
e o *Vou ter um bebé*
eram a ficção científica
que eu mais apreciava
não aceitei o bolo
em forma de coração
que os rapazes
dão às raparigas
no Tirol
até porque não mo deram
as nossas mãos
no escuro do cinema
e no escuro da noite
não eram para ser
partilhadas
imagino-te morto
cheio de sex-appeal
e eu viva
sem sex-appeal nenhum
um dia morro
como tu
a vida não era isto
nós sabíamos
no Céu há muitas moradas
(para nós um duplex certamente)

or in the same city
we never crossed paths
because we couldn't
we looked
for each other
through streaming tears
seeing other people
go out on dates
like it was nothing
I read *Yoga for Pregnant Women*
and *I'm Going to Have a Baby*
they were my favourite
science fiction
I didn't accept
the heart-shaped cake
that the young men
give young women
in Tyrol
nor did anyone offer me one
our hands
in the dark cinema
and in the dark of night
were not to be
joined
I imagine you dead
full of sex appeal
and me alive
with no sex appeal at all
one day I'll die
like you
we both knew
this isn't life
in Heaven there are many mansions
(we'll no doubt have a duplex)

UMA AFIRMAÇÃO DE PESSOA SOBRE MILTON

Não escrevia Milton um verso
sem que o fizesse como se desse verso
dependesse toda a sua fama futura
ela não escrevia um verso

Ela não era Milton

Para poder dizer isto
tinha-lhe sido preciso ler Milton
estudar mais inglês para ler melhor Milton
tentar traduções de Milton e rasgá-las
tentar parafrasear Milton para o comentar
e desistir de o ler
a preocupar-se com Milton
deixou de se preocupar com os seus versos
que ficaram numa lata de bolachas
e ainda lá devem estar
podia ter ido para a província
dar lições particulares de inglês
não diria uma palavra sobre Milton
mas as crianças haviam de repetir
até terem os olhos encarnados
How do you do? What's the weather like today?
mas subitamente começou a dar erros de ortografia
deixou de escrever
versos já não escrevia há anos
mas cartas para recomendar criadas
ainda ia escrevendo
mas a uma criada perguntaram
ao ver a carta de recomendação
se ela tinha trabalhado para uma criada
(a criada ficou fula)
então ela passou a esfregar o chão
numa casa de passe
esfregava o chão lavava as paredes

WHAT PESSOA SAID ABOUT MILTON

"Milton did not write one verse
without writing it as if all
his future fame depended on it"
she did not write one verse

She was not Milton

For her to be able to say the same thing
she would have had to read Milton
to study more English to read Milton better
to make translations of Milton and rip them up
to try paraphrasing Milton so as to comment on him
and to quit reading him
she worried so much about Milton
that she stopped worrying about her own verses
which got left in a cookie tin
and are probably still there
she could have gone to the interior
to give private English lessons
she wouldn't so much as mention Milton
but the children would have repeated
"How do you do? What's the weather like today?"
until their eyes were bloodshot
but she suddenly started making spelling mistakes
and stopped writing
for some years now she hadn't written verses
but she still wrote
reference letters for housemaids
until after seeing her reference letter
someone asked the housemaid who presented it
if her last employer had been a housemaid
(the housemaid was furious)
so she started scrubbing the floor
in a brothel
she scrubbed the floor washed the walls

fazia as camas da casa de passe
sem dizer uma palavra
(se abria a boca gaguejava)
como se chama? um gato comeu-lhe a língua?
perguntavam-lhe os clientes e as prostitutas da casa de passe
quando se lembrava de Milton (mas era raro)
achava os clientes e as prostitutas da casa de passe
mais afáveis do que Milton

EU QUERO FODER foder
achadamente
se esta revolução
não me deixa
foder até morrer
é porque
não é revolução
nenhuma
a revolução
não se faz
nas praças
nem nos palácios
(essa é a revolução
dos fariseus)
a revolução
faz-se na casa de banho
da casa
da escola
do trabalho
a relação entre
as pessoas
deve ser uma troca
hoje é uma relação
de poder

and made the beds in the brothel
without saying a word
(if she opened her mouth she stuttered)
what's your name? did you lose your tongue?
asked the clients and the whores of the brothel
when she thought of Milton (which was rare)
it struck her that the clients and whores of the brothel
were more congenial than Milton

I WANT TO FUCK to fuck
to find joy in fucking
if this revolution
won't let me
fuck till I die
then the revolution
is a lie
the revolution
doesn't happen
in the squares
or in palaces
(that's the revolution
of the Pharisees)
the revolution
happens in the bathroom
at home
at school
at work
the relationship between
people
should be an exchange
today it's a relationship
of power

(mesmo no foder)
a ceifeira ceifa
contente
ceifa nos tempos livres
(semana de 24 x 7 horas já!)
a gestora avalia
a empresa
pela casa de banho
e canta
contente
porque há alegria
no trabalho
o choro da bebé
não impede a mãe
de se vir
a galinha brinca
com a raposa
eu tenho o direito
de estar triste

(even in fucking)
the reaper cheerfully
reaps
she reaps in her free time
(now 24 hours, 7 days a week!)
the manager rates
the company
based on the bathroom
and cheerfully
sings
because there's joy
in the workplace
the crying of the baby
doesn't stop its mother
from coming
the hen plays
with the fox
I have a right
to be sad

DIE WELT VON GESTERN

Eu falo do mundo de ontem, de uma vizinhança
perdida, reparada algures entre as flores breves
do sono. Toco pela manhã, ambas as mãos
compadecidas, a relação dos nossos direitos,
a indefinida memória desses dias vividos
em Salzburg e Viena. No papel escreve-se a palavra
insubmissa, o fragmento que se quis a tudo
sobrevivente, às tardes em Baden e Le Coq,
ao tiro de Sarajevo, o cerco de Leninegrado.

Sob o peso deste céu abrasivo considera,
amor, a paisagem desenhando-se pelo frestão
das nossas venezianas. Elas que pulsando
repetem contra a chuva a dor das nossas vidas.
Junta-lhes o passado, as profecias de Cassandra
e Jeremias, a pequena e inútil maravilha

Paulo Teixeira

Born in 1962, in Maputo (then Lourenço Marques), Mozambique. Moved with family to Portugal in 1974. Earned a degree in Geography and Regional Planning at Lisbon's Universidade Nova [New University] and an M.A. in Geography in Salvador, Brazil. Taught high school in Lisbon and conducted creative writing workshops in public schools around Portugal. DAAD Berlin Artist-in-Residence in 2005. Currently lives in Brazil.

DIE WELT VON GESTERN

I speak of the world of yesterday, of a lost
closeness, glimpsed somewhere amid sleep's
brief flowers. In the morning I touch, with
impassioned hands, the record of our rights,
the hazy memory of our days in Salzburg
and Vienna. On the paper I write the unyielding
word, the vestige intent on surviving
everything: afternoons in Baden-Baden and Le Coq,
the shot at Sarajevo, the siege of Leningrad.

Under the weight of this harsh sky consider,
love, the landscape emerging in the window
of our jalousies, which patteringly repeat
against the rain the sorrow of our lives.
Add to them the past, Cassandra's and Jeremiah's
prophecies, the small and useless suicidal

suicidária que é a Europa. Exilada, remoendo
as palavras que a noite te consente, ensaia,
amor, antes da luz deste veemente crepúsculo
tropical, as palavras destras e desoladas do adeus.

DURANTE O ASSÉDIO A BAGDAD, 813

I
Esqueço-me nos atalhos de outro corpo
enquanto o musgo, o embuste de uma língua,
dissemina raízes pela inanidade da pedra.

II
Tardes de luz declinam à minha volta,
o firmamento, a tenda diáfana onde incrustar,
numa bizarria de pintor, a nova fase da lua.

III
Não há amor que discipline o coração
nem família mais próxima que a do vinho
quando na língua firma um laço de sangue.

IV
Ele em mim clama por uma sombra
mais óbvia que o sono e a noite arqueada
de nuas estátuas sobre o corpo.

V
Um pássaro afaga então os meus olhos,
o lento mover das suas asas, como uma nuvem
se suspende sobre estilhas de madeira em chamas.

marvel called Europe. In this exile, pondering
the words the night allows you, rehearse,
love, before the light of this fierce tropical
twilight, the deft and desolate words of farewell.

DURING THE SIEGE OF BAGHDAD, 813

I

I lose myself in the byways of another body
while the moss, a trick of the tongue,
spreads across the stone's vacancy.

II

Around me fall the glowing evenings,
the diaphanous tent of the heavens inlaid
by the moon's new phase, like a painter's whimsy.

III

There is no love that keeps the heart in line,
no family closer than wine's fellowship
when on the tongue it signs a bond of blood.

IV

He clamours in me for a shadow
weightier than sleep and the night now arching
with naked statues over the body.

V

Then a bird caresses my eyes,
the slow flapping of its wings, like a cloud
hovering over splinters of wood on fire.

VI
O desejo é a nossa árvore genealógica,
a terra que nomeia sua haste vagarosa
no deleite casual de uma palavra nascida em minha boca.

VII
Podia aspirar no seu hálito uma alma
se alma fosse, mais que o odor que passa,
com a presença fascinante da morte a meu lado.

VIII
Agasalhe-o o hábito talar dos meus gestos
ante o medo, com o invasor às portas da cidade,
que o vento escreve numa sentença o seu nome e o meu.

IX
Onde quer que volva agora os meus olhos
levanta-se uma casa. O tempo fez de mim o seu molde
e no ouvido segreda-me que a eternidade podia ser aqui.

AS CRIANÇAS

São crianças que não gostariam de ter nascido.
Patinam sobre o gelo até ao fundo do bosque,
convocando milagres com o olhar, buscando
um rosto na baça luz dos cafés. Cada dedo
é um amuleto a guardá-las do quarto da lua

ou do rebate dos sinos no alto da torre.
Sós, são velhas como as horas no quadrante.
Denunciam com a voz um outro poder,
invisível, sugerido pelas sombras e o medo,
a cidade à noite suspensa de seus braços.

VI
Desire is our genealogical tree,
the earth naming its languid stem
in the chance delight of a word born on my lips.

VII
In your breath I could breathe a soul
if it were a soul, not a passing scent,
with the fascinating presence of death at my side.

VIII
In the face of fear, the invader at the city gates,
let the long robe of my gestures wrap you,
as the wind in one verdict writes your name and mine.

IX
Now wheresoever I turn my eyes
a house is raised. Time made me into its shape,
and whispers in my ear that eternity could be here.

THE CHILDREN

These children wouldn't have wanted to be born.
They skate over the ice deep into the woods,
calling up miracles with their gaze, seeking
a face in the dim light of cafés. Each finger
is a talisman protecting them from the moon's phase

and from the toll of bells in the high tower.
Alone, they're old like the hours of the clock dial.
With their voices they disclose another power,
invisible but suggested by shadows and fear,
the city at night hanging in their arms.

AUTO-DE-FÉ

Quando o amor é como os papéis velhos
e anseia por mais arte que a do poema
o coração é o forno onde ardem as palavras.

*

Nesse dia elas foram, amarradas com barbante,
viúvas precipitando-se dentro da pira.
Fiquei a vê-las abrirem-se como pétalas
para logo definharem a meus olhos
numa florescência não cumprida.
O seu frémito era ainda uma ânsia minha.

Remexi as cinzas, agitei o ar com as mãos.
Vi como um poema se mostra servil ante o fogo.
E pensei: ardessem também os meus dedos!
Para que o poema não deixe crias ao morrer
e não mais confira o direito à vida
do que nele vai escrito.

*

Porque o amor é a arte que fica além do poema,
no dia em que não escrever mais poemas
sei que o amor resgatará o meu corpo da chama.

AUTO-DA-FÉ

When love is like old papers and yearns
for more art than the art of the poem,
the heart is the furnace where words burn.

*

Tied up with string, on that day they were
widows hurling themselves onto the pyre.
I watched them open up like petals,
then dwindle to nothing before my eyes
in their frustrated attempt to flower.
Their quivering was also one of my yearnings.

I stirred the ashes, waved the air with my hands.
I saw how servile a poem is before fire.
And I thought: if my fingers would also burn!
Then the poem would die without offspring
and no longer grant the right to life
to whatever was written in its verses.

*

Since love is an art that thrives beyond poems,
I know that on the day I quit writing them
love will redeem my body from the flames.

A INFÂNCIA DE HERBERTO HELDER

No princípio era a ilha
embora se diga
o Espírito de Deus
abraçava as águas

Nesse tempo
estendia-me na terra
para olhar as estrelas
e não pensava
que esses corpos de fogo
pudessem ser perigosos

Nesse tempo
marcava a latitude das estrelas
ordenando berlindes
sobre a erva

José Tolentino Mendonça

Born in 1965, in Machico, Madeira. Spent his early childhood in Angola, then returned with family to Madeira. Earned a degree in Theology (1989) and a PhD in Biblical Theology at the Portuguese Catholic University of Lisbon (2004), where he is a professor of Biblical Studies and, since 2012, a vice-rector. Also earned a degree in Biblical Sciences at the Pontifical Biblical Institute of Rome (1992). Spent the 2011-12 academic year in New York as a Straus Fellow. Published his first book of poetry in Madeira in 1990, the same year he was ordained a priest. Frequent contributor to periodicals as a commentator on cultural, theological and other topics.

THE CHILDHOOD OF HERBERTO HELDER

In the beginning was the island
although it's said
that the Spirit of God
cradled the waters

In those days
I'd lie on the ground
to look at the stars
without ever thinking
that those bodies of fire
might be dangerous

In those days
I plotted the stars' coordinates
by lining up marbles
on the grass

Não sabia que todo o poema
é um tumulto
que pode abalar
a ordem do universo agora
acredito

Eu era quase um anjo
e escrevia relatórios
precisos
acerca do silêncio

Nesse tempo
ainda era possível
encontrar Deus
pelos baldios

Isto foi antes
de aprender a álgebra

IT'S TIME TO BE CLEAR

Os que falam de mim dizem que sou pobre
Existo à maneira de uma árvore
Tenho diante e atrás de mim a noite eterna
Vacilo, duvido, resvalo
E sei: a maior parte das vezes o amor nasce do erro
transcreve-se a azul ou a negro
sobre passagens, casas inacabadas, alturas remotas

Observá-lo apenas serve
para tornar contundente a sua forma nunca exactamente igual
a sua incrível velocidade destacada no meio do nada
enquanto a noite se desmorona
sempre mais bela

I didn't know that every poem
is a tumult
that can upset
the order of the universe now
I believe

I was almost an angel
and wrote accurate
reports
about silence

In those days
it was still possible
to find God
in the wastes

That was before
I learned algebra

IT'S TIME TO BE CLEAR

Those who notice me say I'm poor
I exist like a tree
Behind and ahead of me lies the eternal night
I vacillate, doubt, slip
And I know: more often than not love is born from error
it is transcribed in blue or black
on crossings, unfinished houses, remote times

Observing it only serves
to accentuate its never exactly equal shape
to isolate its unthinkable speed in the midst of nothing
while the night slowly crashes
forever more beautiful

O ESTERCO DO MUNDO

Tenho amigos que rezam a Simone Weil
Há muitos anos reparo em Flannery O'Connor

Rezar deve ser como essas coisas
que dizemos a alguém que dorme
temos e não temos esperança alguma
só a beleza pode descer para salvar-nos
quando as barreiras levantadas
permitirem
às imagens, aos ruídos, aos espúrios sedimentos
integrar o magnífico
cortejo sobre os escombros

Os orantes são mendigos da última hora
remexem profundamente através do vazio
até que neles
o vazio deflagre

São Paulo explica-o na Primeira Carta aos Coríntios,
«até agora somo o esterco do mundo»,
citação que Flannery trazia à cabeceira

STRANGE EYES

Que revelações nos esperam
sem modo nenhum de compreensão:
o disparo de um comboio
o pensamento aparente
a imagem dos outros nas nossas noites
a simples diferença que nunca é

THE RUBBISH OF THE WORLD

I have friends who pray to Simone Weil
For some years now I've looked to Flannery O'Connor

Prayer must be like those things
we say to someone who's sleeping
we have and don't have any hope
only beauty can come down and save us
when the barriers are lifted
allowing images, noises and spurious
sediments to become part
of the magnificent
pageant on top of the ruins

Those who pray are like beggars of last resort
deeply rummaging through the emptiness
until that emptiness bursts
into flame inside them

St. Paul explains it in the First Letter to the Corinthians,
"we are the rubbish of the world to this very day",
a citation that Flannery kept at her bedside

STRANGE EYES

What revelations await us
without any chance we'll understand:
the hurtling of a train
the startling thought
the image of others visiting our nights
the simple difference that never is

Tão absolutamente só
o nosso coração bate

Um caminho de barro vermelho e poeira
e eu abraçado a ti na grande bicicleta
nunca tirava os olhos dos campos
às vezes avistava um anjo de costas voltadas

Tu dizias
De terra em terra indivisíveis
somos uma coisa que Deus toca

A história será apenas
um indício para a história
um sinal que nos escapa

SALMO JUNTO AO RIO HUDSON

Se fazes sair, a seu tempo, as constelações
e as enumeras com exactidão
Se sabes de que lado habita a luz
e descobres atalhos
para os armazéns do mar
Se te ergues no alto e cavalgas com o vento
muito além do Empire State Building
ou da Freedom Tower em construção

Sobre a terra desolada, peço-te
prepara o caminho onde me vou perder

Absolutely alone
our heart beats

A dusty red-clay path and my arms
wrapped around you on the huge bicycle
I never took my eyes off the fields
sometimes spotting an angel from behind

You said
From land to land all of them connected
we're something that God touches

Each story is only
a clue to the story
a sign that escapes us

A PSALM NEXT TO THE HUDSON RIVER

You who make the constellations appear
in their time and number them all exactly
You who know on which side light dwells
and discover shortcuts
to the oceans' warehouses
You who range the heights and ride with the wind
far above the Empire State Building
or the Freedom Tower under construction

You I ask to prepare the way
where I'll lose myself on this desolate earth.

A POESIA COMPLETA DE MARIANNE MOORE

Uma vida não se compõe de factos e de usos
mas de logro e lenda
Ao cruzar-se com os vizinhos no elevador
Marianne Moore dizia-lhes muitas vezes
quanto o consolo da metafísica pode, por isso,
ser profundo

À data da sua morte
pelo relato indiscreto, mas fiel, da porteira
ficaram a saber que coleccionava:
caixas de cristal e prata, estados de transe,
livros encriptados, ironias, almanaques de basebol,
as portas caídas de Babilónia,
e catálogos de facas artesanais

CALLE PRÍNCIPE, 25

Perdemos repentinamente
a profundidade dos campos
os enigmas singulares
a claridade que juramos
conservar

mas levamos anos
a esquecer alguém
que apenas nos olhou

THE COMPLETE POETRY OF MARIANNE MOORE

A life isn't made up of facts and uses
but of hoaxes and tales
Running into her neighbours in the elevator
Marianne Moore often told them
how the consolation of metaphysics can,
for this reason, be profound

After her death they learned
from the indiscreet but faithful account of the concierge
some of the things she collected:
crystal and silver boxes, states of trance,
encrypted books, ironies, baseball almanacs,
the toppled gates of Babylon,
and catalogues of handmade knives

CALLE PRÍNCIPE, 25

Without warning we lose
the vastness of the fields
singular enigmas
the clarity we swear
we'll preserve

but it takes us years
to forget someone
who merely looked at us

AVE

Uma ave agonizante
entrou-te no quarto,

Apenas uma sombra
que se enlaça
noutra:

assim definiste
a memória,

a cidade
que se mineraliza
quando
rodeias
essa sombra-ave

Luís Quintais

Born in 1968, in Luena (then Luso), Angola. Moved with his family to Lisbon in 1975. Earned a PhD in Social and Cultural Anthropology from the Social Sciences Institute of the University of Lisbon (2005). Has lived since 1995 in Coimbra, where he teaches Anthropology at the University of Coimbra. Blogger and contributor to periodicals on literary, cultural and anthropological topics.

BIRD

A dying bird
entered your bedroom,

just a shadow
merging
into another:

that's how you defined
memory,

the city
which is mineralized
the moment
you surround
that shadow bird

com os dedos
apavorados.

FOR ANIMALS

For animals eternal Treblinka

Está repleta de martírio a memória que me deram.

A mãe levava-me pela mão. O perímetro sacrificial era já ali. O som das aves antecipando o fim, os gorjeios inocentes, a emudecida violência das carcaças expostas, as vísceras, o fedor das vísceras gritando. Fúria e som esgotavam-se em podridões. Em certos ângulos do perímetro bancas clamavam verdade e comércio. Copiosas, as carnes esfoladas surgiam suspensas em metálicos ganchos. Penas e plumas encharcadas pejavam o chão. Uma ave decapitada abraçava o mundo. Em certos pontos do perímetro estreitos canais expulsavam o sangue para um sítio que me pareceu distante, tão distante quanto um país distante.

A gutural agonia apagava-se. Fechavam-se as cortinas para a tranquila refeição do meio-dia.

O MUNDO COMO REPRESENTAÇÃO

"O mundo é a minha representação."
Que tipo de imagem
eclode na mente
quando, de noite, um cão uiva,
como se a sua carne
não fosse carne da sua carne,
mas um véu espesso
que cobre a dor
e a torna mais intensa?

with your terrified
fingers.

FOR ANIMALS

For animals eternal Treblinka

The memory I've been given is rife with martyrdom.

Mother took me by the hand. We had reached the sacrificial perimeter. The sound of chickens facing the end. Their innocent clucking. The hushed violence of exposed carcasses. Guts, the stench of screaming guts. Fury and sound collapsed into rottenness. There were stands within the perimeter calling for truth and commerce. The plump, flayed meats lightly swayed, hanging from large metal hooks. Soaked feathers littered the ground. A decapitated chicken embraced the world. Narrow furrows inside the perimeter carried off the blood to a place I imagined to be far away, as far as a faraway country.

The guttural agony subsided. People were drawing their drapes for the peaceful midday meal.

THE WORLD AS REPRESENTATION

"The world is my representation."
What sort of image
flashes in my mind
when a dog howls in the night
as if its flesh
were not flesh of its flesh
but a thick veil
covering its pain
and making it sharper?

Uma janela abre-se de par em par,
e eu persigo os sulcos e a ira
desse cão mirífico,
desse cão que existe algures
para lá do ver.

A noite que ignorei torna-se visível,
mas não a ira, a ira absoluta do cão,
ainda que os meus olhos
ceguem numa exasperante vontade
de luz.

DO GELO

para J.G. Ballard

À psicologia profunda tudo devemos.
Acima de todas as coisas, devemos-lhe
o que não comunica, o que a inocência
e o esquecimento traem.
É à ímpia hipótese que tudo devemos:
a do negro icebergue evolutivo
que no cérebro espelha abominações
e que nos faz balbuciar o seu fogo
e o seu reino.

As lições do gelo são a melhor explicação
da arte das cesuras e dos caprichos:
o que não fará certamente a cidade,
o que não compõe um segredo
que não seja a plena paixão do ilegível.

I fling open a window
and pursue the trail and rage
of that preternatural dog,
that dog that exists somewhere
beyond seeing.

The night I'd ignored becomes visible,
but not that rage, that dog's absolute rage,
even if my eyes go blind
from searching, with a desperate will,
for light.

ON ICE

for J.G. Ballard

To deep psychology we owe everything.
We owe to it more than anything else
whatever doesn't communicate, whatever
innocence and forgetfulness let slip.
We owe everything to this ungodly hypothesis:
the evolutionary black iceberg
which mirrors abominations in the brain
and makes us sputter its fire
and its kingdom.

The lessons of ice are the best explanation
for the art of caesuras and of whims:
things that will certainly not make a city,
things that will not form a secret
unless it's the pure passion of the illegible.

ECOLALIA

Uma fúria secular faz-me fugir
das múltiplas vozes
de um só deus.

Está repleto de vestígios
este mundo, de ecos
que antepassados esclarecem
        equivocamente.

O indeterminado ofício
destes ecos repete-se
sem que eu pressinta o padrão,
        o desarme e a nitidez.

Vi o meu pai chorar
e o que me vence desde aí
é o eco do seu choro

repetindo-se nos versos lidos,
roubados por vocação sem medida:
uma janela abre-se para a pobre noite

da carne tomada de assalto pela linguagem.
Vejo o meu pai através dessa janela.
A linguagem inventada dilacera-me.

É uma música do passado,
uma marca-de-água
no meu sistema nervoso.
Os significados são exteriores ao círculo
que me inclui.
Persigo-os, porém.

ECHOLALIA

An ancient fury makes me flee
from the multiple voices
of the same god.

This world teems with
vestiges, with echoes
that ancestors equivocally
        clarify.

The indefinite oration
of these echoes keeps repeating
without me discerning their disarming
        pattern and precision.

I saw my father cry
and what still haunts me today
is the echo of his crying

repeated in verses I read and steal
by vocation, without measure:
a window opens on to the poor night

of flesh overpowered by language.
I see my father through that window.
The invented language tears me to pieces.

It's a song from the past,
a watermark
in my nervous system.
The meanings are outside the circle
that contains me.
Even so, I pursue them.

SUBJECTIVAS MESAS

(sobre Wallace Stevens)

É com uma estranha malícia
que distorço o mundo.
Assim se revigora o opaco
e a possibilidade de invenção, ainda.

O cimento é o tonal modo
de nos agarrar às significativas paisagens
a ocidente.

Dobram-se como árvores, as frases,
sob o vento que veio do nada.
Asas destroem a insaciada ordem
que nos governa, a polis de anátema
que se instala no texto.

Vejamos: a cidade começa aqui
nas ásperas figuras do entardecer.
Descrevo o que flutua
neste espaço, a infigurável

destreza moderna trucidando
com dedos de morte
os acantos e as cicutas

que só existem em reais palavras
como subjectivas mesas
sobre as quais me desloco,
velozmente.

SUBJECTIVE TABLES
(on Wallace Stevens)

It is with a strange malice
that I distort the world.
Thereby reinvigorating the opaque
as well as the possibility of invention.

Cement is the tonal mode
for binding us to significant landscapes
in the West.

Sentences bow like trees
under the wind that came from nowhere.
Wings destroy the insatiable order
that rules us, the polis of anathema
that spreads into the text.

Observe: the city begins here
in the sharp shapes of late afternoon.
I describe what hovers
in this space, the unrepresentable

modern dexterity slaughtering
with fingers of death
the acanthi and the hemlocks

that only exist in real words
as subjective tables
over which I swiftly
glide.

PROCURO O TRÂNSITO de um homem que repousa em ti
Como se desvia um homem do seu coração para seguir viagem
Como deixa ficar tudo e acrescenta à sua herança

Procuro conhecer os símbolos, os marcos miliares
Diurnos, como se lêem
Sinais de fumo e o ângulo dos pombos — e todas as coisas
Que nos chegam da distância

Procuro saber como se fecham os pés dentro dos teus
Percursos
Como se põe descalço um homem que necessita
De atravessar-se
E desejo outra vez desdobrada a tua palavra cheia
De estrelas

Para que as recorte, para que as ponha no silêncio
Vivas

Daniel Faria

1971-1999. Born in Baltar, a town in northern Portugal. Attended seminary schools (1983-94) and then the Portuguese Catholic University of Oporto, where he earned a degree in Theology (1996). Simultaneously pursued a degree in Portuguese Studies (obtained in 1998) at the University of Oporto. Following a call to be a monk, he became a postulant in 1997 but died from a hard fall towards the end of his novitiate year at a Benedictine monastery. Literary and contemplative, he also devoted time to community service.

I SEEK THE PATH of a man who rests in you
As a man deserts his heart to journey onward
As a man leaves everything and adds to his inheritance

I seek to know symbols, the milestones
Seen in daylight, how to read
Smoke signals and the arc of pigeons — and all
Things that reach us from the distance

I seek to keep my feet naturally within your
Roads
As a man removes his shoes to cross himself
Like a stream
And I long for your word bursting once more
With stars

So that I can cut them out and place them in the silence
Alive

Na minha boca e nas minhas mãos
Em chamas

ESCREVO DO LADO mais invisível das imagens
Na parede de dentro da escrita e penso
Erguer à altura da visão o candeeiro
Branco da palavra com as mãos

Como a paveia atrás do segador
Vejo os pés descalços dos que correm
E escrevo para os que morrem sem nunca terem provado o pão
Grito-lhes: imaginai o que nunca tivestes nas mãos

Correi. Como o segador seguindo o segador
Numa ceifa terrestre, tombando. Digo:
Imaginai

1
JÁ ME ENSINARAM que o sol
Não morre. Eu acredito
Na noite (o meu coração morre às escuras)

2
É verdade que acredito ho homem
Que não fala (no homem que comunica
Com as mãos). Acredito
Na dor reveladora das coisas decepadas

3
É verdade que estou muito triste
Na terra (já me indicaram a estrada
Com luz pública). Estou sentado nos degraus
Como alguém que parou de subir

In my mouth and in my hands
On fire

I WRITE ON THE MOST INVISIBLE side of images
On the inside wall of writing and I think
Of lifting with my two hands
The white lamp of the word to the height of vision

Like the haystack behind the harvester
I see the bare feet of those who run
And I write for those who die without ever tasting bread
I shout to them: imagine what your hands never held

Run! Like the harvester following the harvester
In an earthly harvest, falling. I say:
Imagine

1
I HAVE BEEN TAUGHT that the sun
Doesn't die. I believe
In the night (my heart dies in the dark)

2
It is true that I believe in the man
Who doesn't talk (in the man who speaks
With his hands). I believe
In the revelatory pain of things severed

3
It is true that I am exceedingly sad
On earth (I have been shown the way
With public lighting). I'm sitting on the steps
Like someone who has stopped climbing

UM PÁSSARO EM QUEDA mesmo
Quando é proporcional à pedra
Que tomba do muro nunca
Alcança a mesma coloração do musgo
— Já nem sequer falo do tempo
Em que mudam a pena

Para fazeres ideia pensa
Como perde um homem a idade
De encontrar os ninhos

Retém na memória: o homem cai. Desloca-se
O pássaro para que as estações não mudem

É dessa rotação que o muro
Pode cercar-se sem ninguém o construir. O cerco
Do voo é a pedra da idade

Para fazeres uma ideia pensa
Em engoli-la

O meu projecto de morrer é o meu ofício
Esperar é um modo de chegares
Um modo de te amar dentro do tempo

DO CICLO DAS INTEMPÉRIES

1
Sabes leitor, que estamos ambos na mesma página
E aproveito o facto de teres chegado agora
Para te explicar como vejo o crescer de uma magnólia.
A magnólia cresce na terra que pisas — podes pensar
Que te digo alguma coisa não necessária, mas podia ter-te dito,
acredita,

A BIRD IN FREE FALL even
When equal in size to the stone
That falls from the wall will never
Attain the same colouring as the moss
And much less so in the time
When birds change their feathers.

To have some idea think
Of how a man loses the age
Of when he looked for nests

Keep in mind: man sinks. The bird keeps
Moving so that the seasons don't change.

It is by that rotation that the wall can be
Circled without anyone building it. The circle
Of flight is the stone of age

To have some idea think
Of swallowing it

Dying is my project and my vocation
Waiting is my way for you to arrive
My way of loving you inside time

THE CYCLES OF BAD WEATHER

1

We are on this page together, reader, and I am going
To take advantage of the fact you have come here
To tell you how a magnolia tree grows, as I see it.
The magnolia grows in the ground you walk on. You may think
I am telling you something useless, but I could have said, believe me,

Que a magnólia te cresce como um livro entre as mãos. Ou melhor,
Que a magnólia — e essa é a verdade — cresce sempre
Apesar de nós.
Essa raiz para a palavra que ela lançou no poema
Pode bem significar que no ramo que ficar desse lado
A flor que se abrir é já um pouco de ti. E a flor que te estendo,
Mesmo que a recuses
Nunca a poderei conhecer, nem jamais, por muito que a ame,
A colherei.

A magnólia estende contra a minha escrita a tua sombra
E eu toco na sombra da magnólia como se pegasse na tua mão.

2

Quero dizer-te que esta magnólia não é a magnólia
Do poema de Luiza Neto Jorge que nunca veio
A minha casa — ela própria dava flor
Ela riscava nas folhas
Ela era grande mesmo quando a magnólia não crescia

Esta magnólia não é como a dela uma magnólia pronunciada
É uma magnólia de verdade a todo o redor — maior
E mais bonita do que a palavra.

4

Se te puseres à escuta a magnólia pode ser uma árvore de fruto —
A escuta enche-nos de sumo como um poço no meio dos pátios.
A magnólia enxerta-me nos pensamentos, é um profundo
Rumor na minha carne, a linha que me vai da mão
A outra mão. Ela não tem medo
De aproximar-se quando minha mãe me pega ao colo.
Ela levanta-me da terra
Como os tufões e os bandos dos pássaros.

That the magnolia grows like a book in your hands. Or I could
have said
That the magnolia — and this is the truth — keeps growing
In spite of us.
The word-root that the tree has brought into the poem
Might well signify that the flower blooming on the branch
On your side is already a little of you. And even if you refuse
The flower I offer you, I can't ever know it, nor will I ever pluck it,
However much I love it.

The magnolia casts your shadow against my writing
And I touch the magnolia's shadow as if grasping your hand.

2

I want you to know that this magnolia is not the magnolia
Of the Luiza Neto Jorge poem that never came
To my house — it flowered on its own
It wrote across the pages
It was great even when the magnolia did not grow

This magnolia is not like hers a pronounced magnolia
It is a true magnolia in all its circumference — greater
And more beautiful than the word.

4

If you listen closely the magnolia can be a fruit tree.
Close listening fills us with juice like a well in a courtyard.
The magnolia grafts into my thoughts, it is a deep
Rumble in my flesh, the line connecting my one hand
To the other. It is not afraid
Of coming close when my mother holds me in her lap.
It lifts me up from the earth
Like typhoons or flocks of birds.

5

Começo, pois, no alto a saciar-te. Explico-te o ciclo
Das intempéries e das migrações. Se puderes ficar em silêncio
Não te igualarás à magnólia, mas repousarás
Como o musgo que lhe cresce no tronco.
És tu que cresces, afinal. És tu que sobes
— Mesmo se já abandonaste a minha infância —
Aos ramos que te ofereço. Dou-te também
Poder para a arrancares deste poema
Ou até de toda a minha terra interior
E de a transplantares noutros lugares — nos versos seguintes.
Se a guardares como um tesouro verás como brilha
Como acende a pulsação dos pássaros — o seu canto,
Da ida e da vinda, aos teus ouvidos.

7

Magoa ver a magnólia cair. Acredita.
O relâmpago vem
Sobre ela. A tempestade.
As plantas são tão frágeis como as cabanas dos homens.
Somos muito frágeis os dois neste poema
Com o relâmpago, a cabana, com a magnólia aos ombros
Sem nenhum terreno pulmonar intacto
Para depois de nos olharmos um de nós dizer
Plantêmo-la aqui — *aqui*
É o meu pulso, a minha boca
É a retina com que procuras, é a madeira da porta
Com que te fechas em casa. Prometo-te
Eu nunca vou fechar os olhos
As mãos.

5

And I start filling you from on high, explaining the cycles
Of bad weather and migrations. If you can keep silent
You will not equal the magnolia, but you will rest
Like the moss that grows on its trunk.
In fact you are the one growing. You are the one climbing
— Even if you have already deserted my childhood —
To the branches I offer you. I also give you the power
To uproot it from this poem
Or even from my entire inner earth
And to transplant it elsewhere — in subsequent verses.
If you cherish it like a treasure you will see how it shines
How it ignites the birds' throbbing — their song,
As they come and go, in your ears.

7

It hurts to see the magnolia fall. Believe me.
Lightning
Hits it. The storm.
Plants are as fragile as the cabins of men.
Both of us are very fragile in this poem
With lightning, a cabin, and a magnolia on our shoulders
And no pulmonary ground firm enough
For one of us to say, after looking into each other's eyes,
Let's plant it here — *here*
Is my pulse, my mouth
Is the retina of your searching, is the wood in the house door
You pull shut with yourself inside. I promise you
Never will I shut these eyes
These hands.

AS JUSTAS PARTILHAS

brutalmente frugal o que levaste:
a mais sobraram umas falhas
falta luz digo falta espaço
disseste como se fora
o que sempre te faltou mas
o tempo igualmente se esgotou
e não há penalização
por tudo
nem se compensam as manchas
do nada
que resta e acastanhece na casa
e que me não cabe e
se dantes coube nunca
eu soube dissolver.

Margarida Vale de Gato

Born in 1973, in Vendas Novas, south-central Portugal. Studied at the University of Lisbon, where she earned several degrees, including a PhD in North American Literature and Culture (2008). A dedicated translator of fiction and poetry, she also teaches translation at the University of Lisbon. Regularly publishes literary criticism and essays on translation.

EQUITABLE DIVISION

what you took was brutally frugal:
too many gaps are what remained
not enough light I say not enough room
you said as if that were what
you'd always been lacking but
time also ran out on us
and there's not a penalty
for everything
nor a payback for the mildew
of this nothing
that lingers greying in the rooms
and doesn't fit me and even
if it used to fit I never
learned how to dissolve it

A IMAGEM ROMÂNTICA

Há outras coisas, Horácio,
e a tua filosofia é barata,
na verdade não custa fixar
as coisas ideais à distância:
terás vista panorâmica
mas sempre a visão é polémica.

Gostava que alguém me mostrasse,
mas não terei nunca garantia
de que envelhecer faça sentido.

As pessoas prostram-se, queremos que nos digam
porquê não haver luz nos seus rostos. Crestam
os cravos, antes rubros. Não há modo
de saber se as monarcas
têm memórias arenosas de lagarta.
Tudo sucede dentro de estanques
casulos, a seda é densa,
não se faz ideia
se isto acaba. Estrelas foscas
correm, pessoas morrem, a vida
é breve, impávido o
real se esquiva a designar.
Comparar é colidir: o verbo
talvez nos leve
a mais nenhum sinal.

COM PAIXÃO E HIPOCONDRIA

Confortamo-nos com histórias laterais,
evitamos o toque, há risco de contágio;
por mais que preservemos a franqueza

THE ROMANTIC IMAGE

There are more things, Horatio,
and your philosophy's cheap,
it doesn't take much to capture
ideal things from a distance:
you get a panoramic view
but the vision is always debatable.

I'd like someone to show me,
but I can never be sure
there's a meaning to growing old.

People start drooping, we want them to tell us
why there's no light in their faces. The reddest
carnations wither. There's no way
to know if monarchs
have sandy caterpillar memories.
Everything happens in hermetic
cocoons, the silk's wound tight,
we've no idea
if this ends. Dim stars
hurtle, people die, life
is brief, undaunted
reality eludes designation.
To compare is to collide: the word
might lead us
to no further sign.

WITH PASSION AND HYPOCHONDRIA

We take comfort in external affairs,
avoiding contact, it could be contagious;
however guileless we've remained,

passou o estágio já da frontal alegria:
estamos bem, obrigada, embora aquém
de antes — entretanto admitimos não
saber, e enquanto resta isto indefinido,
mesmo com luvas, pinças de parafina,
não sondamos mais, sob pena de crescer
um quisto nesse incisivo sítio onde
achámos sem tacto que menos doía.

MEDEIA

[Lugar baixo, rancor surdo, tremenda
raiva — o despeito da mulher
ao centro e o sensato coro atrás.]

Diz-se que matou o próprio irmão,
que descende do Sol e solo bárbaro,
e que, deslumbrada por jovem prático
e pouco espiritual, lhe deu
um animal de lã dourada. Ele
porém ainda quis um trono, outro
matrimónio e o mando dum país.

Quando uma feiticeira chora invoca
demónios que invocam malefícios.
O escritor, atento ao móbil, fixa
os joelhos da semideusa mágica
e empático pinta-lhe na boca
a palavra trágica: eu nada quis
para mim, por ti só tudo fiz.

E o mundo entretém no seu decurso
o público. Do crime participa
quem dele tira prémio ou espanto —

the stage of outright happiness has passed:
we're fine, thank you, though less than
we were, but we admit we're not really
sure, and as long as this uncertainty lasts,
not even with gloves and paraffin pincers
will we probe any further, lest a cyst
erupt in that delicate spot where we
thought it would hurt less by not touching.

MEDEA

[Low-lying place, seething rancour, high
rage — the resentment of the woman
in the centre and the wise chorus behind.]

They say she killed her own brother,
descends from the Sun and barbarian soil,
and gave an animal with golden fur
to a practical, not very spiritual young man
who had taken her breath away. But he
also wanted a throne, a second
wife and a country to rule.

When a sorceress weeps she invokes
demons who invoke curses.
The writer, aware of her motive, steadies
the knees of the magic demigoddess
and empathically paints on her mouth
the tragic words: I wanted nothing
for myself, I did it all for you.

And the course of the world entertains
the audience, the crime's accomplices,
those it profited and those it petrified.

E o pranto corre a cada livre gesto
e o excesso com que sofre nos consola
o sobressalto. E o manto que tece
sufoca em chamas e excita deveras
o sangue a correr e a carne a arder.

Resta um par de cadáveres infantis
aos pés do pai: o céu está vazio
e ninguém saiu ainda da sala.
Para concluir o acto o génio
declara solene que ali se ama
e mata sobre a cena. Não mais
discursos. Inclina-se e repousa

a pena com a ponta de veneno.

And tears roll with each free motion,
and the acuteness of her suffering softens
our shock. The cloak she weaves
smothers with flames, and the spurting
blood and burning flesh truly excite us.

What remains is a pair of infant corpses
at their father's feet: the sky is empty
and no one has yet left the hall.
To conclude the act the genius
solemnly declares that there, on stage,
people love and kill. No more
speeches. He leans back and sets down

his pen with its poisonous nib.

VELHO MESTRE

O silêncio
de um fruto sobre a mesa,
apenas ferido
por um gume de luz
no meridiano.

Mas nenhuma ameaça,
nem o arnês de dedos
formando-se no horizonte,
apenas o golpe de sol
afiado na vidraça.

Um fruto
é um velho mestre
esperando na luz
as trevas
do amadurecimento.

Daniel Jonas

Born in 1973, in Oporto. Earned a degree in Modern Languages and Literatures (English and Portuguese) at the University of Oporto (1999) and a master's degree in Literary Theory at the University of Lisbon (2006). Schoolteacher of Portuguese and History in Oporto. Collaborates in theatre productions as a playwright, translator (of Shakespeare, Pirandello...) and director. Also translates poetry and prose.

OLD MASTER

The silence
of a fruit on the table,
bruised only
by a blade of light
across its meridian.

But nothing threatens,
not even the grapnel of fingers
hovering on the horizon,
just the whetted sun
striking the window.

A fruit
is an old master
waiting in the light
for the darkness
of maturity.

CASAS

As casas. Sonho com as casas.
Sonho com as casas de dentro
e passo pelas casas habitando-as por fora
e penso que as casas são sentenças
que me condenam à liberdade.

As casas. Sonho com as casas.
Gostava de as habitar a todas
e a cada uma delas
e a voar com as asas de dentro
visitante de outras vidas,
vivendo-as e não se me fecharem
como uma blusa ao olhar que se lhes atira
de passagem,
estores que caem como ghilhotinas
decapitando o horizonte.

Eu sinto o coração das casas
e voo-me para delas dentro
como um pássaro que mergulhe na vidraça
e entre num azul mais penetrante.

As casas. Sonho com as casas.
Observo-as e por instantes
são minhas e minhas todas
as vidas que eu ensaio
porque de mim sempre me saio.
As casas. Condenam-me a não serem minhas.
Bah! Condeno-as a não terem asas.

HOUSES

Houses. I dream of houses.
I dream of houses on the inside
and live in them on the outside, passing by
and I think houses are sentences
condemning me to freedom.

Houses. I dream of houses.
I'd like to live in them all
and in each one of them
and to fly with wings on the inside
as a visitor to other lives,
living them without them closing up on me
like a coat buttoned up against
a passing glance
or roller shutters lowered like guillotines
beheading the horizon.

I feel the heart of houses
and fly into their interiors
like a bird diving into the window
to enter a more penetrating blue.

Houses. I dream of houses.
I observe them and for brief moments
they're mine along with all
the lives I keep trying
since I never stop leaving me.
Houses. They condemn me to their not being mine.
Bah! I condemn them to not having wings.

UM LAMENTO

Oh, como aquele coelho coxeando além
a lenta deserção das coisas,
a estranheza súbita do íntimo,
a intimidade súbita do estranho!

Não encontres o teu fim no teu princípio,
fim no teu fim.
Aquele coelho há-de continuar cambaleante
parecendo escapado à tua cartola
para dentro da vegetação

e tu, deixado sob o tule das libélulas
como um soldado ferido
sob as pás de inatingíveis helicópteros,
hás-de perguntar porque partiram coisas
que eram tuas

e ali mesmo
no idílio do lugar
com o arrebol sangrando sobre
os teus ombros
recordar a formatura,
o distante primeiro beijo das coisas
ou certo de um consolo existencial
a ti próprio antes do gesto decisivo,
do sabor sem caroço do mirtilo

que mordesses
como o estalido
que despoletasse
sonolenta mina.

A LAMENT

Like that rabbit limping away
oh the slow desertion of things,
the sudden strangeness of the intimate,
the sudden intimacy of the strange!

Don't find your end in your beginning,
the end in your end.
That rabbit will keep hobbling,
like an escapee from your hat,
into the brush

while you, sprawled under the dragonflies' tulle
like a wounded soldier
under the wings of oblivious helicopters,
will ask why things that were yours
departed

and right there
in the idyll of that moment
with the twilight bleeding over
your shoulders you'll think back
to your conscription, to your commencement,
to that long-ago first kiss of things
or, counting on an existential consolation,
to you yourself before that fateful act,
that seedless taste of the blueberry

which you bit
like the click
that set off
a sleeping mine.

OS DIAS DECLINANDO

Tudo o que um dia te foi belo e amplo e prometedor
reúne-o e faz dele forragem e um telhado
para os teus dias inglórios de colmo

porque não haverá um dia um único
que não te aponte as graves falhas do que és
com a lanterna do esplêndido assomo do que foras.

Eu sei-o. Vou olhando-os fixamente nos olhos,
mosca aprisionada na cozedura da teia,
como repentino encontro com um velho conhecido
que julgara não se haver perdido de vista.

THE DECLINING DAYS

Gather whatever in your life was one day beautiful
large and promising and make it into fodder and a roof
for your inglorious days of thatch

for there will not be a day not one
that doesn't point out awful flaws in what you are
with the lamp of the glowing image of what you were.

I know. I look at them all straight in the eyes,
a fly imprisoned in this simmering web,
as if I'd suddenly run into an old acquaintance
I thought I hadn't lost track of.

NOTES TO THE POEMS

p. 39, FROM MY WINDOW
Albert Samain (1858-1900) was a French Symbolist poet much admired by Espanca.

p. 95, BEING BEAUTEOUS
The title is borrowed from a poem by Rimbaud.

p. 121, *"The lover transforms into the thing loved"*
This is the opening verse of a famous sonnet by Luís de Camões.

p. 159, LAMENT FOR DIOTIMA
In Plato's *Symposium*, Socrates talks about (Platonic) love by quoting at length what he learned from Diotima, a philosopher and priestess of Mantinea.

p. 199, HISTORICAL TRUTH
Caldas da Rainha, a town located about fifty miles north of Lisbon, is famous for its glazed pottery.

p. 201, ALL SO FRAGILE
Definite and indefinite articles in Portuguese are gendered. The "articles in the dark" of the final verse stress the fact that the sexual identity of the lovers in the poem is unknown, and irrelevant.

p. 215, *I want to fuck to fuck*
The neologism *achadamente*, from the second verse of the poem in Portuguese, is an adverb derived from *achada*, "found". The poet explained to me that she meant something like *alegremente* (joyfully), *com gratidão* (gratefully) or *agradecidamente* (thankfully).

p. 219, DIE WELT VON GESTERN
The German means "The World of Yesterday" and is the title of Stefan Zweig's autobiography, completed on the day before he and his second wife committed suicide in Brazil, in 1942. The "record of our rights", in the fourth verse, seems to refer to the opening paragraphs of the biography, where Zweig recounts how, in pre-World War I Austria, individual rights were specifically set out by law.

POET BIBLIOGRAPHIES

Editions of selected or collected poems in Portuguese are listed only if they include previously unpublished work.

ALBERTO CAEIRO

Poetry Collections: *O Guardador de Rebanhos* (containing forty-nine poems, about half of which were published in the Lisbon magazine *Athena*, in 1925); *O Pastor Amoroso* (eight love poems); *Poemas Inconjuntos* (about seventy miscellaneous poems, sixteen of which were published in *Athena*).

Poetry in English: *The Keeper of Sheep*, tr. Edwin Honig and Susan M. Brown (Riverdale-on-Hudson, New York: Sheep Meadow Press, 1986); *Sheep's Vigil by a Fervent Person*, tr. Erin Mouré (Toronto: House of Anansi Press, 2001); *The Collected Poems of Alberto Caeiro*, tr. Chris Daniels (Bristol: Shearsman Books, 2007); *Alberto Caeiro: The Complete Poems*, tr. Michael Lee Rattigan (Toronto: Rufus Books, 2007).

RICARDO REIS

Poetry Collections: *Odes – Livro Primeiro* (1924). This first book of twenty odes, published in the magazine *Athena*, was supposed to be followed by others, but while some two hundred additional odes were written, they were never organized into books.

ÁLVARO DE CAMPOS

Poetry Collections: *Livro de Versos* was one of various working titles for Campos's poetry, but no actual book ever took shape.

Poetry in English: *The Collected Poems of Álvaro de Campos*, vol. 2, tr. Chris Daniels (Bristol: Shearsman Books, 2007).

FERNANDO PESSOA

Poetry Collections: *Antinous* (1918), *35 Sonnets* (1918), *Poetry I-II-III*, in 2 vols. (1921), *Mensagem* (1934). (The first three titles are chapbooks of his poetry in English.) Had plans to publish his prolific output of poems under titles such as *Cancioneiro* [Songbook] and *Itinerário* [Itinerary], but these never materialized.

Authored many posthumously published prose works, including the *Livro do Desassossego* [Book of Disquiet].

Poetry in English: *Selected Poems of Fernando Pessoa*, tr. Edwin Honig (Chicago: Swallow Press, 1971); *Fernando Pessoa: Sixty Portuguese Poems,* tr. F.E.G. Quintanilha (Cardiff: University of Wales Press, 1971); *Selected Poems,* tr. Peter Rickard (Edinburgh: Edinburgh University Press, 1972); *Selected Poems*, tr. Jonathan Griffin (London: Penguin, 1982); *Poems of Fernando Pessoa*, tr. Edwin Honig and Susan M. Brown (New York: Ecco Press, 1986; San Francisco: City Lights Books, 1998); *Self-analysis and Thirty Other Poems*, tr. George Monteiro (Providence: Gávea-Brown, 1989); *Message*, tr. Jonathan Griffin (London: Menard Press, 1992; Bristol: Shearsman Books, 2007); *Fernando Pessoa & Co. – Selected Poems*, tr. Richard Zenith (New York: Grove Press, 1998); *Selected Poems*, tr. David Butler (Dublin: Dedalus Press, 2004); *A Little Larger Than the Entire Universe – Selected Poems of Fernando Pessoa*, tr. R. Zenith (New York & London: Penguin, 2006); *Message*, tr. R. Zenith (Lisbon: Oficina do Livro, 2008); *Forever Someone Else: Selected Poems*, tr. R. Zenith (Lisbon: Assírio & Alvim, 2008).

FLORBELA ESPANCA

Main Poetry Collections: *Livro de Mágoas* (1919), *Livro de Sóror Saudade* (1923), *Charneca em Flor* (1931; published one month after her death).

Other, posthumously published works include juvenilia, miscellaneous poems, short stories, letters, and a diary.

JORGE DE SENA

Main Poetry Collections: *Perseguição* (1942), *Coroa da Terra* (1946), *Pedra Filosofal* (1950), *As Evidências* (1955), *Fidelidade* (1958), *Post-Scriptum* [in *Poesia I*] (1961), *Metamorfoses* (1963), *Arte de Música* (1968), *Peregrinatio ad Loca Infecta* (1969), *Exorcismos* (1972), *Camões Dirige-se aos Seus Contemporâneos e Outros Textos* (1973), *Conheço o Sal e Outros Poemas* (1974), *Sobre esta Praia... Oito Meditações à Beira do Pacífico* (1977), *40 Anos de Servidão* (1979), *Sequências* (1980), *Visão Perpétua* (1982), *Post-Scriptum II* (1985), *Dedicácias* (1999).

Also authored short stories, a novel, a novella, plays, and a large body of literary studies. Various volumes of letters exchanged with other writers have also been published.

Poetry in English: *Over this Shore... Eight Meditations on the Coast of the Pacific*, tr. Jonathan Griffin (Santa Barbara: Mudborn Press, 1979); *The Poetry of Jorge de Sena*, ed. Frederick G. Williams, various translators (Santa Barbara: Center for Portuguese Studies, Univ. of Calif. at Santa Barbara, 1980); *In Crete with the Minotaur and Other Poems*, tr. George Monteiro (Providence: Gávea-Brown, 1980); *Art of Music*, tr. Francisco Cota Fagundes and James Houlihan (Huntington, West Virginia: University Editions, 1988); *Metamorphoses*, tr. Francisco Cota Fagundes and James Houlihan (Providence: Copper Beech Press, 1991); *The Evidences*, tr. Phyllis Sterling Smith (Santa Barbara: Center for Portuguese Studies, Univ. of Calif. at Santa Barbara, 1994).

SOPHIA DE MELLO BREYNER ANDRESEN

Main Poetry Collections: *Poesia* (1944), *Dia do Mar* (1947), *Coral* (1950), *No Tempo Dividido* (1954), *Mar Novo* (1958), *O Cristo Cigano* (1961), *Livro Sexto* (1962), *Geografia* (1967), *Dual* (1972), *O Nome das Coisas* (1977), *Navegações* (1983), *Ilhas* (1989), *Musa* (1994), *O Búzio de Cós e Outros Poemas* (1997).

Published collections of short stories, several plays, children's stories, and essays.

Poetry in English: *Marine Rose: Selected Poems*, tr. Ruth Fainlight (Redding Ridge, Conn.: Black Swan Books, 1986); *Log Book*, tr. Richard Zenith (Manchester: Carcanet Press, 1997).

CARLOS DE OLIVEIRA

Main Poetry Collections: *Turismo* (1942), *Mãe Pobre* (1945), *Colheita Perdida* (1948), *Descida aos Infernos* (1949), *Terra de Harmonia* (1950), *Cantata* (1960), *Sobre o Lado Esquerdo* (1968), *Micropaisagem* (1968), *Entre Duas Memórias* (1971), *Pastoral* (1977).

Published five novels.

Poetry in English: *Guernica and Other Poems*, tr. Alexis Levitin (Toronto: Guernica Editions, 2004).

EUGÉNIO DE ANDRADE

Main Poetry Collections: *Adolescente* (1942), *Pureza* (1945), *As Mãos e os Frutos* (1948), *Os Amantes sem Dinheiro* (1950), *As Palavras Interditas* (1951), *Até Amanhã* (1956), *Coração do Dia* (1958), *Mar de Setembro* (1961), *Ostinato Rigore* (1964), *Obscuro Domínio* (1971), *Véspera da Água* (1973), *Escrita da Terra* (1974), *Homenagens e Outros Epitáfios* (1974), *Limiar dos Pássaros* (1976), *Memória Doutro Rio* (1978), *Matéria Solar* (1980), *O Peso da Sombra* (1982), *Branco no Branco* (1984), *Vertentes do Olhar* (1987), *Contra a Obscuridade* (1988), *O Outro Nome da Terra* (1988), *Rente ao Dizer* (1992), *Ofício de Paciência* (1994), *O Sal da Língua* (1995), *Pequeno Formato* (1997), *Os Lugares do Lume* (1998), *Os Sulcos da Sede* (2001).

Published several volumes of prose pieces, children's literature, and translations.

Poetry in English (all translated by Alexis Levitin): *Inhabited Heart: The Selected Poems of Eugénio de Andrade* (Los Angeles: Perivale Press, 1985); *White on White* (Princeton: Quarterly Review of Literature, 1987); *Memory of Another River* (Minneapolis: New Rivers Press, 1988); *The Slopes of a Gaze* (Tallahassee: Apalachee Press, 1992); *Solar Matter* (Fort Bragg, N. Car.: QED Press, 1995); *Shadow's Weight* (Providence: Gávea-Brown, 1996); *Another Name for Earth* (Fort Bragg: QED Press, 1997); *Dark Domain* (Toronto: Guernica Editions, 2000); *Close to Speech* (Lancaster, Calif.: Red Dancefloor Press, 2000); *Forbidden Words* (New York: New Directions, 2003).

MÁRIO CESARINY DE VASCONCELOS

Main Poetry Collections: *Corpo Visível* (1950), *Discurso sobre a Reabilitação do Real Quotidiano* (1952), *Louvor e Simplificação de Álvaro de Campos* (1953), *Manual de Prestidigitação* (1957), *Pena Capital* (1957), *Alguns Mitos Maiores e Alguns Mitos Menores Postos à Circulação pelo Autor* (1958), *Nobilíssima Visão* (1959), *Planisfério e Outros Poemas* (1961), *A Cidade Queimada* (1965), *O Virgem Negra* (1989).

Also published essays, criticism, and poetic prose.

ALEXANDRE O'NEILL

Main Poetry Collections: *Tempo de Fantasmas* (1951), *No Reino da Dinamarca* (1958), *Abandono Vigiado* (1960), *Poemas com Endereço* (1962), *Feira Cabisbaixa* (1965), *De Ombro na Ombreira* (1969), *Entre a Cortina e a Vidraça* (1972), *A Saca de Orelhas* (1979), *As Horas Já de Números Vestidas* (1981), *Dezanove Poemas* (1983), *O Princípio de Utopia, O Princípio de Realidade seguidos de Ana Brites, Balada Tão ao Gosto Popular Português & Vários Outros Poemas* (1986).

ANTÓNIO RAMOS ROSA

Main Poetry Collections: *O Grito Claro* (1958), *Viagem Através de uma Nebulosa* (1960), *Voz Inicial* (1960), *Sobre o Rosto da Terra* (1961), *Ocupação do Espaço* (1963), *Estou Vivo e Escrevo Sol* (1966), *A Construção do Corpo* (1969), *A Pedra Nua* (1972), *O Ciclo do Cavalo* (1975), *Boca Incompleta* (1977), *A Nuvem sobre a Página* (1978), *Círculo Aberto* (1979), *O Incêndio dos Aspectos* (1980), *Declives* (1980), *O Centro na Distância* (1981), *O Incerto Exacto* (1982), *Quando o Inexorável* (1983), *Gravitações* (1983), *Dinâmica Subtil* (1984), *Mediadoras* (1985), *Volante Verde* (1986), *Clareiras* (1986), *No Calcanhar do Vento* (1987), *O Livro da Ignorância* (1988), *O Deus Nu(lo)* (1988), *Três Lições Materiais* (1989), *Acordes* (1989), *O Não e o Sim* (1990), *Facilidade do Ar* (1990), *Oásis Branco* (1991), *Intacta Ferida* (1991), *A Rosa Esquerda* (1991), *Clamores* (1992), *Lâmpadas com Alguns Insectos* (1992), *O Teu Rosto* (1994), *Delta seguido de Pela Primeira Vez* (1996), *A Mesa do Vento seguido de As Espirais de Dioniso* (1997), *Versões/Inversões* (1997), *Pátria Soberana seguido de Nova Ficção* (1999), *O Princípio da Água* (2000), *As Palavras* (2001), *O Aprendiz Secreto* (2001), *Deambulações Oblíquas* (2001), *O Deus da Incerta Ignorância seguido de Incertezas ou Evidências* (2001), *O Sol é Todo o Espaço* (2001), *Os Volúveis Diademas* (2002), *Cada Árvore é um Ser para Ser em Nós* (2002), *O Que Não Pode Ser Dito* (2003), *Relâmpago de Nada* (2004), *Passagens* (2004), *Génese seguido de Constelações* (2005), *Horizonte a Ocidente* (2007), *Em Torno do Imponderável* (2012), *Numa Folha, Leve e Livre* (2013).

HERBERTO HELDER

Main Poetry Collections: *A Colher na Boca* (1961), *Poemacto* (1961), *Lugar* (1962), *Electronicolírica* (1964; subsequently retitled *A Máquina Lírica*), *Humus* (1967), *Retrato em Movimento* (1967), *Vocação Animal* (1971), *Poesia Toda* (1973; collected poetry to date, including some poems previously unpublished in book form; in successive editions of the work, the author has kept adding poems from new collections, but some poems — whether older or newer — he excludes), *Cobra* (1977), *O Corpo, o Luxo, a Obra* (1978), *Photomaton & Vox* (1979), *Flash* (1980), *A Cabeça entre as Mãos* (1982), *Última Ciência* (1988), *Os Selos* (1990), *Os Selos, Outros, Últimos* (1991), *Do Mundo* (1994), *Doze Nós numa Corda* (1997), *A Faca Não Corta o Fogo* (2008), *Servidões* (2013), *A Morte sem Mestre* (2014).

Has published short stories and collections of poems from other languages "changed" (to use his way of saying "very loosely translated") into Portuguese.

RUY BELO

Main Poetry Collections: *Aquele Grande Rio Eufrates* (1961), *O Problema da Habitação* (1962), *Boca Bilingue* (1966), *Homem de Palavra[s]* (1970), *Transporte no Tempo* (1973), *A Margem da Alegria* (1974), *Toda a Terra* (1976), *Despeço-me da Terra da Alegria* (1977).

Also published essays, and translations from the work of Saint-Exupéry, García Lorca, Borges and others.

FIAMA HASSE PAIS BRANDÃO

Main Poetry Collections: *Morfismos* (1961), *Barcas Novas* (1967), *(Este) Rosto* (1970), *O Texto de João Zorro* (1974; includes first three collections and a fourth collection, titled *Era*), *Novas Visões do Passado* (1975), *Homenagem à Literatura* (1976), *Melómana* (1978), *Área Branca* (1978), *Âmago: Nova Arte* (1985), *Três Rostos* (1989), *Obra Breve* (1991; collected poetry, including previously unpublished poems; enlarged edition 2006), *Cantos do Canto* (1995), *Epístolas e Memorandos* (1996), *Cenas Vivas* (2000), *As Fábulas* (2002).

Published plays, essays and translations of Solomon's *Song of Songs* and works by Novalis, Artaud, Brecht, Updike and others.

LUIZA NETO JORGE

Main Poetry Collections: *A Noite Vertebrada* (1960), *Quarta Dimensão* (1961), *Terra Imóvel* (1964), *O Seu a Seu Tempo* (1966), *Dezanove Recantos* (1969), *Os Sítios Sitiados* (1973), *A Lume* (1989).

Published many translations, including works by Sade, Verlaine, Céline and Yourcenar.

VASCO GRAÇA MOURA

Main Poetry Collections: *Modo Mudando* (1963), *Semana Inglesa* (1965), *Quatro Sextinas* (1973), *O Mês de Dezembro e Outros Poemas* (1976), *Recitativos* (1977), *Sequências Regulares* (1978), *Instrumentos para a Melancolia* (1980), *A Variação dos Semestres deste Ano, 365 Versos, seguido de A Escola de Frankfurt (1981), Nó Cego, o Regresso* (1982), *Os Rostos Comunicantes* (1984), *A Sombra das Figuras* (1985), *A Furiosa Paixão pelo Tangível* (1987), *O Concerto Campestre* (1993), *Sonetos Familiares* (1995), *Uma Carta no Inverno* (1997), *Poemas com Pessoas* (1997), *O Retrato de Francisca Matroco e Outros Poemas* (1998), *Sombras com Aquiles e Pentesileia* (1999), *Testamento de VGM* (2001), *Variações Metálicas* (2004), *Laocoonte, Rimas Várias, Andamentos Graves* (2005), *O Caderno da Casa das Nuvens* (2009).

Published novels, novellas, short stories, criticism, and translations of Dante, Petrarch, Shakespeare (the sonnets) and more recent poets.

ANTÓNIO FRANCO ALEXANDRE

Main Poetry Collections: *Sem Palavras nem Coisas* (1974), *Os Objectos Principais* (1979), *Visitação* (1983), *A Pequena Face* (1983), *As Moradas 1 & 2* (1987), *Oásis* (1992), *Poemas* (1996; collected poetry to date, including *Terceiras Moradas* and other previously unpublished poems), *Quatro Caprichos* (1999), *Uma Fábula* (2001), *Duende* (2002), *Aracne* (2004).

AL BERTO

Main Poetry Collections: *À Procura do Vento num Jardim d'Agosto* (1977), *Meu Fruto de Morder, Todas as Horas* (1980), *Trabalhos do*

Olhar (1982), *O Último Habitante* (1983), *Salsugem* (1984), *A Seguir o Deserto* (1984), *Três Cartas da Memória das Índias* (1985), *Uma Existência de Papel* (1985), *O Medo* (1987; collected work to date, including poems not yet published in book form; expanded editions published in 1991 and 1998), *O Livro dos Regressos* (1989), *A Secreta Vida das Imagens* (1991), *Canto do Amigo Morto* (1991), *Luminoso Afogado* (1995), *Horto de Incêndio* (1997).

Published several volumes of prose texts.

Poetry in English: *The Secret Life of Images*, tr. Richard Zimler (Dublin: Mermaid Turbulence, 1997).

NUNO JÚDICE

Main Poetry Collections: *A Noção de Poema* (1972), *O Pavão Sonoro* (1972), *Crítica Doméstica dos Paralelepípedos* (1973), *As Inumeráveis Águas* (1974), *O Mecanismo Romântico da Fragmentação* (1975), *Nos Braços da Exígua Luz* (1976), *O Corte na Ênfase* (1978), *O Voo de Igitur Num Copo de Dados* (1981), *A Partilha dos Mitos* (1982), *Lira de Líquen* (1985), *A Condescendência do Ser* (1988), *Enumeração de Sombras* (1989), *As Regras da Perspectiva* (1990), *Uma Sequência de Outubro* (1991), *Um Canto na Espessura do Tempo* (1992), *Meditação sobre Ruínas* (1994), *O Movimento do Mundo* (1996), *A Fonte da Vida* (1997), *Raptos* (1998), *Teoria Geral do Sentimento* (1999), *Poesia Reunida 1967-2000* (2001; collected poetry to date, including previously unpublished work), *Pedro Lembrando Inês* (2001), *Cartografia de Emoções* (2002), *O Estado dos Campos* (2003), *Geometria Variável* (2005), *Geografia do Caos* (with photographs by Duarte Belo) (2005), *As Coisas mais Simples* (2006), *A Matéria do Poema* (2008), *O Breve Sentimento do Eterno* (2008), *Guia de Conceitos Básicos* (2010).

Has published fictional works, plays, and literary criticism.

Poetry in English: *Meditation on Ruins*, tr. R. Zenith (Prague: Archangel Books, 1997); *The Cartography of Being*, tr. Paulo da Costa (Amazon Digital Services: Livros Pé d'Orelha, 2012).

ANA LUÍSA AMARAL

Main Poetry Collections: *Minha Senhora de Quê* (1990), *Coisas de Partir* (1993), *Epopeias* (1994), *E Muitos os Caminhos* (1995), *Às*

Vezes o Paraíso (1998), *Imagens* (2000), *Imagias* (2002), *A Arte de Ser Tigre* (2003), *A Génese do Amor* (2005), *Entre Dois Rios e Outras Noites* (2007), *Se Fosse um Intervalo* (2009), *Vozes* (2013), *Escuro* (2014).

Has published children's stories, a verse play and a novel.

ADÍLIA LOPES

Main Poetry Collections: *Um Jogo Bastante Perigoso* (1985), *O Poeta de Pondichéry* (1986), *A Pão e Água de Colónia* (1987), *O Marquês de Chamilly* (1987), *O Decote da Dama de Espadas* (1988), *Os 5 Livros de Versos Salvaram o Tio* (1991), *Maria Cristina Martins* (1992), *O Peixe na Água* (1993), *A Continuação do Fim do Mundo* (1995), *Clube da Poetisa Morta* (1997), *Sete Rios entre Campos* (1999), *Florbela Espanca Espanca* (1999), *Irmã Barata, Irmã Batata* (2000), *Obra* (2000; collected poetry to date, including the previously unpublished *O Regresso de Chamilly*), *A Mulher-a-Dias* (2002), *César a César* (2003), *Poemas Novos* (2004), *Le vitrail la nuit e A Árvore Cortada* (2006), *Caderno* (2007), *Apanhar Ar* (2010), *Andar a Pé* (2013).

Has published a short collection of fables.

PAULO TEIXEIRA

Main Poetry Collections: *As Imaginações da Verdade* (1985), *Conhecimento do Apocalipse* (1988), *A Região Brilhante* (1988), *Inventário e Despedida* (1991), *Arte da Memória* (1992), *O Rapto de Europa* (1994), *Patmos* (1994), *As Esperas e Outros Poemas* (1997), *Túmulo de Heróis Antigos* (1999), *Autobiografia Cautelar* (2001), *Orbe* (2005), *O Anel do Poço* (2009).

JOSÉ TOLENTINO MENDONÇA

Main Poetry Collections: *Os Dias Contados* (1990), *Longe Não Sabia* (1997), *A Que Distância Deixaste o Coração* (1998), *Baldios* (1999), *De Igual para Igual* (2001), *A Estrada Branca* (2005), *Tábuas de Pedra* (2005; with art work by Ilda David'), *O Viajante sem Sono* (2009), *Estação Central* (2012), *A Papoila e o Monge* (2013).

Has published theological works and several plays.

LUÍS QUINTAIS
Main Poetry Collections: *A Imprecisa Melancolia* (1995), *Lamento* (1999), *Umbria* (1999), *Verso Antigo* (2001), *Angst* (2003), *Duelo* (2004), *Canto Onde* (2006), *Mais Espesso que a Água* (2008), *Riscava a Palavra Dor no Quadro Negro* (2010), *Depois da Música* (2013), *O Vidro* (2014).

DANIEL FARIA
Main Poetry Collections: *Uma Cidade com Muralha* (1991), *Oxálida* (1992), *A Casa dos Ceifeiros* (1993), *Explicação das Árvores e Outros Animais* (1998), *Homens que São Como Lugares Mal Situados* (1998), *Dos Líquidos* (2000), *Poesia* (2003; collected poetry, including juvenilia and previously unpublished work).

MARGARIDA VALE DE GATO
Main Poetry Collections: *Mulher ao Mar* (2010), *Mulher ao Mar Retorna* (2013; enlarged version of previous book).

Has published book-length translations of works by Poe, Dickens, Wilde, Christina Rossetti, Yeats, René Char, and others.

DANIEL JONAS
Main Poetry Collections: *O Corpo Está com o Rei* (1997), *Moça Formosa, Lençóis de Veludo* (2002), *Os Fantasmas Inquilinos* (2005), *Sonótono* (2007), *Passageiro Frequente* (2013), *Nó* (2014).

Has published a play and numerous translations, including a Portuguese rendering of Milton's *Paradise Lost.*

ACKNOWLEDGEMENTS

All translations in this volume are under copyright. Copyright to the original Portuguese poems — except those by Fernando Pessoa and Florbela Espanca, whose work is in the public domain — is vested in the poets or their heirs and sometimes in their publishers as well.

All living poets personally authorized the publication of the poems included; when necessary, permission was also obtained from their agents / representatives and publishers. Authorizations were likewise secured from the heirs, agents and publishers of deceased poets. We are deeply grateful to the poets and to those who hold rights in their work for the permissions granted. We are particularly grateful to SPA (Sociedade Portuguesa de Autores) for their assistance in obtaining many of these permissions.

Every effort has been made to trace copyright holders of the poems included in this volume. The editors and publisher apologize for any errors or omissions in the clearing of these permissions, and, upon receipt of written notice from the copyright holder, will undertake to make good any such errors or omissions in all future editions.

With the exception of poems of Fernando Pessoa and his heteronyms, and those of Florbela Espanca — the original editions of which are long since out of print — the following list records the original sources of the poems gathered herein.

Jorge de Sena (1919–1978) Dangers of Innocence ("Os Perigos da Inocência", from *Exorcismos*, 1972); Thanksgiving ("Acção de Gracas", from *Post-scriptum*, *Poesia 1*, 1960); At Fifty ("Aos Cinquenta Anos", from *Quarenta Anos de Servidão*, 1979); In Praise of Italy ("Em Louvor da Itália", from *Sequências* 1980); Siegfried's Funeral March ("Marcha Fúnebre de Siegfried, do *Crepúsculo do Deuses*", from *A Arte de Música*, 1968); Desired Tomb ("O Desejado Túmulo", from *Visão Perpétua*, 1982). Grateful thanks to Mécia de Sena.

Sophia de Mello Breyner (1919–2004) Beach ("Praia", from *Coral*, 1950); Lusitania ("Lusitânia", from *Mar Novo*, 1958); I Listen ("Escuto", from *Geografia*, 1967); The Hospital and the Beach ("O Hospital e a Praia", from *Livro Sexto*, 1962); Antinous ("Antínoo", from *Geografia*, 1967); Torso ("Torso", from *O Nome das Coisas*, 1977); The Minotaur ("O Minotauro", from *Dual*, 1972); We Will Rise ("Ressurgiremos", from *Livro Sexto*, 1962). Grafteful thanks to Maria Andresen & Jordi Roca (Mertin Agency).

Carlos de Oliveira (1921–1981) Stalactite (first 7 of 24 sections that make up "Estalactite", from *Micropaisagem*, 1968). Grateful thanks to Porto Editora/Assírio & Alvim.

Eugénio de Andrade (1923–2005) Inhabited Body ("Corpo Habitado", from *Obscuro Domínio*, 1971); Voyage ("Viagem", from *As Palavras Interditas*, 1951); It's a place in the south, a place where ("É um lugar ao sul, um lugar onde", from *Branco no Branco*, II); The houses enter the water ("As casa entram pela água", poem XLIX in *Branco no Branco*, 1984); I don't know what a water-flower is ("Ignoro o que seja a flor da água", poem XVII in *Branco no Branco*, 1984); Upon the table the fruit burns: pears ("Sobre a mesa a fruta arde: peras", poem XXVI in *Branco no Branco*, 1984); Just the horse, just those wide ("Só o cavalo, só aqueles olhos grandes", poem X in *Branco no Branco*, 1984);

Counterpoint ("Contraponto", from *Sulcos da Sede*, 2001); The Fruit ("Os Frutos", from *Ostinato Rigore*, 1964); Other Rhythms, Other Modes ("Outros Ritmos, Outros Modos", from *Sulcos da Sede*, 2001). Grateful thanks to Eugénio de Andrade Foundation. The poems: The houses enter the water, The Inhabited Body and Voyage by Eugenio de Andrade, translated by Alexis Levitin, from *Forbidden Words*, copyright ©1995 by Eugenio de Andrade; translation 1995, 2003 by Alexis Levitin. Reprinted by permission of New Directions Publishing Corp.

Mário Cesariny (1923–2006) poem ("poema" [Faz-se luz pelo processo], from *Pena Capital*, 1957); you are welcome to elsinore ("*you are welcome to elsinore*", from *Pena Capital*, 1957); Ship of mirrors ("O navio de espelhos", from *A Cidade Queimada*, 1965); poem ("poema" [Tu estás em mim como eu estive no berço], from *Pena Capital*, 1957); being beauteous ("*being beauteous*", from *Pena Capital*, 1957). Grateful thanks to Porto Editora/Assírio & Alvim.

Alexandre O'Neill (1924–1986) Standing at Fearful Attention ("Perfilados de Medo", from *Poemas com Endereço*, 1962); History of Morality ("A História da Moral", from *De Ombro na Ombreira*, 1969); Portugal ("Portugal", from *Feira Cabisbaixa*, 1965); Door to Door ("De Porta em Porta", from *Abandono Vigiado*, 1960); Turkey ("Peru", from *As Horas Já de Números Vestidas*, 1981); Lament of a Man who Misses being Blind ("Lamúria do Cego que Antes o Fosse", from *Feira Cabisbaixa*, 1965); First Serious Warning ("Primeira Advertência Séria", from *Entre a Cortina e a Vidraça*, 1972).

António Ramos Rosa (1924–2012) All poems from *Livro da Ignorância*, 1988. Grateful thanks to Maria Filipe Rosa.

Herberto Helder (*b.* 1930) Preface ("Prefácio", from *A Colher na Boca*, 1961); «Transforma-se o amador na coisa amada» ("The lover transforms into the thing loved", from *A Colher na Boca*, 1961); Seated Theory (II) ("Teoria Sentada (II)", from *Lugar*, 1962); it's too late for love, glory or Abyssinia ("já não tenho tempo para ganhar o amor, a glória ou a Abissínia", from *Servidões*, 2013).

Ruy Belo (1933–1978) And Everything was Possible ("E Tudo era Possível", from *Homem de Palavra(s)*, 1970); Pilgrim and Guest on Planet Earth ("Peregrino e Hóspede sobre a Terra", from *Transporte no Tempo*, 1973); Oh Houses Houses Houses ("Oh as Casas as Casas as Casas", from *Homem de Palavra(s)*, 1970); Requiem for a Dog ("Requiem por um Cão", from *Transporte no Tempo*, 1973); Reckoning and Report ("Relatório e Contas", from *Boca Bilingue*, 1966); Hand to the Plough ("A Mão no Arado", from *O Problema da Habitação*, 1962). Grateful thanks to Teresa Belo.

Fiama Hasse Pais Brandão (1938–2007) Still-Life with Praying Mantis ("Natureza Morta com Louvadeus", from *Três Rostos*, 1989); In Praise of the Locust ("Louvor do Gafanhoto", from *Obra Breve*, 1991); I write like an animal, but with less ("Escrevo como um animal, mas com menor", from *Área Branca*, 1979); I bore through the ground to make way ("Furo o chão para dar passagem", from *Área Branca*, 1979); Song of Places ("Canto dos Lugares", from *Cantos do Canto*, 1995); Song of Genesis ("Canto do Génesis", from *Cantos do Canto*, 1995). Grateful thanks to João Cruz.

Luiza Neto Jorge (1939–89) Houses I, II, V, IX, XII, XIII ("As Casas" I, II, V, IX, XII, XIII, from *Terra Imóvel*, 1964); A Magnolia ("A Magnólia", from *O Seu a Seu Tempo*, 1966); The House of the World ("A Casa do Mundo", from *O Seu a Seu Tempo*, 1966).

Vasco Graça Moura (1942–2014) lament for diotima ("lamento por diotima", from *O Concerto Campestre*, 1993); the coffee mill ("o moinho de café", from *Poemas com Pessoas*, 1997); a dog for pompeii ("um cão para pompeia", from *A Furiosa Paixão pelo*

Tangível, 1987); in the manner of the eighteenth century ("A Sequência da Baleia/ I. maneiras oitocentistas", from *O Concerto Campestre*, 1993); fanny ("fanny", from *Poemas com Pessoas*, 1997).

António Franco Alexandre (*b.* 1944) All poems from *As Moradas 1 & 2*, 1987. Grateful thanks to Porto Editora/Assírio & Alvim.

Al Berto (1948-1997) Salt Spray 2, 3, 4 ("Salsugem 2, 3, 4" from *Salsugem*, 1984).

Nuno Júdice (*b.* 1949) All poems taken from *Meditação sobre Ruínas*, 1994.

Ana Luísa Amaral (*b.* 1956) Historical Truth ("A Verdade Histórica", from *Minha Senhora de Quê*, 1990); All So Fragile ("Coisas de Partir", from *Coisas de Partir*, 1993); I'm Going to Load Time ("Irei Agora Carregar o Tempo", from *Se Fosse um Intervalo*, 2009); Palimpsest ("Palimpsesto", from *Vozes*, 2011); The Victory of Samothrace ("A Vitória de Samotrácia", from *Vozes*, 2011).

Adília Lopes (*b.* 1960) Two Cypresses ("Dois Ciprestes", from *Florbela Espanca Espanca*, 1999); What Pessoa Said about Milton ("Uma Afirmação de Pessoa sobre Milton", from *O Decote da Dama de Espadas (Romances)*, 1988) ; I want to fuck to fuck ("Eu quero foder foder", from *Florbela Espanca Espanca*, 1999).

Paulo Teixeira (*b.* 1962) Die Welt von Gestern ("Die Welt von Gestern", from *Inventário e Despedida*, 1991); During the Siege of Baghdad, 813 ("Durante o Assédio a Bagdad, 813", from *Arte da Memória*, 1992); The Children ("As Crianças", from *As Esperas e Outros Poemas*, 1997); Auto-da-fé ("Auto-de-fé", from *Autobiografia Cautelar*, 2001).

José Tolentino Mendonça (*b.* 1965) The Childhood of Herberto Helder ("A Infância de Herberto Helder", from *Os Dias Contados*, 1990); Strange Eyes ("Strange Eyes", from *De Igual para Igual*, 2001); It's Time to be Clear ("It's Time to be Clear", from *Estação Central*, 2012); The Rubbish of the World ("O Esterco do Mundo", from *A Estrada Branca*, 2005); A Psalm Next to the Hudson River ("Salmo Junto ao Rio Hudson", from *Estação Central*, 2012); The Complete Poetry of Marianne Moore ("A Poesia Completa de Marianne Moore", from *Estação Central*, 2012); Calle Príncipe, 25 ("Calle Príncipe, 25", from *Baldios*, 1999). Grateful thanks to Porto Editora/Assírio & Alvim.

Luís Quintais (*b.* 1968) Bird ("Ave", from *Mais Espesso que a Água*, 2008); For Animals ("For Animals", from *Duelo*, 2004); The World as Representation ("O Mundo como Representação", from *Duelo*, 2004); On Ice ("Do Gelo", from *Mais Espesso que a Água*, 2008); Echolalia ("Ecolalia", from *Mais Espesso que a Água*, 2008); Subjective Tables ("Mesas Subjectivas", from *Mais Espesso que a Água*, 2008).

Daniel Faria (1971–1999) I seek the path of a man who rests in you ("Procuro o trânsito de um homem que repousa em ti", from *Dos Líquidos*, 2000); I write on the most invisible side of images ("Escrevo do lado mais invisível das imagens", from *Dos Líquidos*, 2000); I have been taught that the sun ("Já me ensinaram que o sol", from *Dos Líquidos*, 2000); A bird in free fall even ("Um pássaro em queda mesmo", from *Dos Líquidos*, 2000); Dying is my project and my vocation ("O meu projecto de morrer é o meu ofício", from *Explicação das Árvores e de Outros Animais*, 1998); The Cycles of Bad Weather (1, 2, 4, 5, 7) ("Do ciclo das intempéries (1, 2, 4, 5, 7)", from *Dos Líquidos*, 2000). Grateful thanks to Porto Editora/Assírio & Alvim and Comissão de Edição de Daniel Faria.

Margarida Vale de Gato (*b.* 1973) Equitable Division ("As Justas Partilhas", from *Mulher ao Mar*, 2010); The Romantic Image ("A Imagem Romântica", from *Mulher ao Mar*, 2010); With Passion and Hypochondria ("Com Paixão e Hipocondria", from *Mulher ao Mar*, 2010); Medeia ("Medea", from *Mulher ao Mar Retorna*, 2013).

Daniel Jonas (*b.* 1973) All poems from *Passageiro Frequente*, 2013.

CPSIA information can be obtained
at www.ICGtesting.com
Printed in the USA
BVHW081232140120
569353BV00003B/190/P